VICTORIA:

WITH OTHER POEMS.

BY SAREPTA IRISH HENRY.

CINCINNATI:
PUBLISHED BY POE & HITCHCOCK.

R. P. THOMPSON, PRINTER.
1865.

VICTORIA;

OR,

THE TRIUMPH OF VIRTUE.

VICTORIA.

CHARACTERS OF THE POEM.

ERNEST RAYMOND.

VICTORIA, his adopted Daughter.

RUTH, his Housekeeper.

THORNTON RAYMOND, at first as a Stranger.

HERTHA, an Invalid—Wife of Thornton Raymond.

HERTHA'S MOTHER.

CLEONE, betrothed Lover of Victoria.

VICTORIA.

Light is sown for the righteous,
And gladness for the upright in heart. PSALMS.

SCENE I.

ERNEST AND VICTORIA.

Ernest. Victoria!
Victoria. Ay, father, I am here.
Ernest. Your hand, my child; I 've sat here in this bower,
And listened to the murmur of the waves
Upon the sanded shore, until my soul
Has grown into their music—till they seem
Like kindred worshipers, inviting me
To join their evening song of praise; and now
I fain would take the old, accustomed seat
Beneath the vine that overshades the beach,
And, with your voice to cheat my blindness, gaze

Upon the scene that at this hour doth lie
Transfigured 'neath the smile of heaven; and bring
Your harp, and we will concert with the winds,
And birds, and rustling leaves, and chanting waves,
To bear the sweet Day to her rest, with song.

Victoria. A sweet day, sweetly closing! O, there is
To me a sacredness about the hour
Of eventide that all my spirit awes
To quietude. All other hours seem made
For labor; this for rest, and holy thought,
And calm communion with the pure—
A daily Sabbath time.

This holy hour
And this sweet scene suggest a dream of heaven.
'T is sunset on the waters; all is still.
The shores afar lie girt with bands of gold;
The forests are ablaze with shifting fires;
The sapphire waves are calm, and o'er them hangs
The setting sun, while clouds, like heaps of foam
Dashed from the sea of light, lie quivering near.
The pulses of the sea beat soft and still,
And the low murmur of their beating winds
Along the sounding shore in melody.
A song of joy the dreaming waters sing—

A love-song to the clear, departing day,
Beneath the soft effulgence of whose beams
The waters are transfigured; every wave
Doth bear the semblance of the sun, and with
A freight of amethyst and gold floats on,
And breaks among the purple shadows of
The shore. The sun hath set; his latest ray
Doth crown the forest, while the darkness creeps,
With stealthy tread, where late his footsteps lay.
The golden threads are raveled from the waves;
The crimson glories fade; broader the shades
Of purple spread their royal folds; the sky
Grows grander, mirrored in the darkling depths;
A star hangs trembling in the tinted west,
And decks the brow of an uplifted wave;
And Night, the beautiful, glides o'er the sea.

Ernest. A lovely scene! Its beauty penetrates
Beyond my blindness to that inner sense,
Most subtile in its nature, that God gave
Instead of outward vision, and I feel
The glory that my eyes may not behold.

Victoria. Father, I would thou wert not blind!

Ernest. Ay, child,
'T is sad to have the sun, and moon, and stars
From your own heaven blotted out, while yet

O'er kindred worlds they shine so fair. 'T was thus
In bitterness I thought, until I learned
'T was but the hand of God that shaded o'er
My eyes, in loving kindness, from the light,
That, else, had been too strong for me to bear;
That hid, within his palm, the world that had
Eclipsed the glory of his face to me;
That let me walk in darkness, to behold
His starry firmament of love and truth.
And so I am e'en thankful for my lot.
'T is blest with thee, dear child, to guide my steps,
And with thy sight supply my dreary want.

Victoria. The moon glides o'er the hill, the type of peace,
Serene and beautiful, "a thing of joy."
Her beams fall through the vines above thy head,
Wreathing a halo 'mid thy silver hairs,
That gives a prophet's seeming to thy form.

A Voice. If prophet he, spirit art thou, fair maid.

Ernest. Didst thou not hear a voice, my child?

Victoria. I did.
Perhaps some neighbors passing by. But come;
The evening air grows chill, and I will wait
Till thou art seated in thy chair, before
I sing to thee. *(They walk toward the house.)*

Our cottage from between
The overtwining vines gleams in the light
Of the enchanting moon, like some sweet scene
Of fairy land.

Ernest. It is a happy home
To thee, my child?

Victoria. Ay, father, thou art here.
Old Ruth hath placed the lamp upon the stand
Beside the holy Book, for evening prayer,
And waits us, busy with her knitting work—
Industrious soul!

Ernest. And faithful she hath been
These many years, a servant rare to me—
An almost mother to my orphaned child. (*They enter.*)

A Stranger. (*Looking after them from the beach.*)
A scene of fairy-land! a scene of heaven
To me it seems, and I a spirit lost,
Who may not enter there. These several days
I 've hovered round this spot, straining my eyes
If, haply, I might catch one blessed glimpse
Of the within, like furies round the gates
Of Paradise, thirsting for evermore
For one cool drop of its celestial joys.

I wonder if the walls have still the same
Home-look that I remember yet so well;

If still the picture of the thorn-crowned Christ,
Whose calm, sad gaze oft checked my childish mirth,
And woke my heart to pity and to love,
Hangs o'er the old, carved, oaken mantle-tree.
O, those were happy days; for innocent
Love lulled us to our slumbers every night,
And woke us, with her holy kiss, each morn,
Blessing the hours of labor and repose.
I dare not ask how many still are left
Of those who formed the fireside group at eve
In that sweet time; for years have passed, and years
Bring death and change—far more have brought to me
Sin and eternal woe.
But who were they
Who sat so late on this familiar seat?
The white-haired man, of patriarchal mien,
And that fair girl, who, as the moonlight fell
On her white robe and dark and flowing curls,
Seemed as an angel minister to him?
Some guests, perhaps—perhaps—O, can it be
They all are dead? and the old place hath passed
To strangers, who can never understand
The tales these trees, and vines, and blooming shrubs,
And murmuring waters have to tell?

O, thought
Of sorrow! One more pang, to make my life
A throb of agony! I 'll go to-night,
And, with the cold eyes of the moon to mock
My self-wrought misery, count o'er their graves.

SCENE II.

VICTORIA AND RUTH.

Victoria. He sleepeth, Ruth, and if he wake and call
For me, pray tell him I have gone awhile
To Mistress Thornton, sick in Lonesome Dell.
Ruth. 'T is a wild path for you to track alone.
Victoria. I have no fear, good Ruth; I know the way.
Cleone and I have wandered often there;
We found the sweetest berries in its shade;
The finest nuts lay gleaming 'mong the leaves
That fell, with softest music, from its trees,
And rarest flowers grew in the meadow-grass.
I love the path; 't is one of pleasantness;
And then, thou knowest well, duty and love
Will make a rough path smooth. My ever kind
And faithful teacher, she, by patient care,
Hath won my gratitude. My love she stole
By the sweet magnetism of her eye,
Or some most subtile charm of her deep soul

My tongue can not explain. An influence sweet,
And strange as sweet, seems drawing all my soul
To union with her own, whene'er I touch
Her hand, or listen to her voice, or find
Her soft eyes, looking into mine. And now
That she is ill, I feel it is my right
To minister to her such comfort as
May enter, with my presence, her lone room.

Ruth. Go, then, my child; mind well the path; return
Again before the eventide. But stay!
Take thou this flask of wine, like water, pure
From all that poisons human blood or brain,
(My own hands pressed it from the ripened fruit,)
As a small token of my sympathy
For one who suffers, with my hopeful wish
That God may soon, in love, restore her health.
See how the wine, in its soft-coloring, keeps
A memory of the rosy, Summer dawns
From out whose honeyed dews these juices rare
Were gathered and were perfected.

Victoria. Thanks, Ruth,
I thank thee in her stead. Adieu. (*Departs.*)

Ruth. (*Watching her from the door.*) Sweet child!
The old man's heart is in her tiny hand,

Like to some crystal vase of antique mold,
Where, 'mid the leaves of withered blooms, there
grows
One solitary flower—his love for her.
Should aught of evil overtake her steps,
Her hand would hold a broken heart.

Victoria. (*In a woodland path.*)

O, it is sweet to go away alone
In Nature's solitudes, and, 'neath the vast,
Empyrean dome of her own temple grand,
Worship the God to whom her altars are
Upreared, to honor whom she offers up
Her hourly, daily, yearly sacrifice
Of beauty and of song.
Whoe'er hath stood
Between the everlasting, pine-clad hills,
That rise above the shadows of the earth
Into the calm, unclouded light of heaven,
And listened to the tones outrolling from
Their caverns deep and grand, like organ swells,
Blent with the sweeter sounds of bird and wave,
And hath not felt within his wondering soul
That the eternal God was there revealed,
Until the eye suffused and throbbing heart
Gave token of his power? Who hath not felt

At such a time, in such a place, his soul
Expand, until its greatness seemed to fill
The universe, and reach the throne of God?
  I seem akin to God to-day—akin
To all created things. These hills and trees
My brothers are, these flowers my sisters sweet,
Nature my mother kind and true, and God
The Father of us all—a blessed band!
  It thrills my deepest soul to feel the calm,
Great heart of Nature, filled to overflow
With the quick essence of the life of joy
Beating so near to mine. How every leaf
And every flower seems trembling with the bliss
That pulses through its every vein! I love
These days, this tuneful month of June, so glad
With song. I love this wrinkled earth; each nook
And corner of the grand old thing is dear,
Because God made it, and because it is
So old.
            'T is a grand place to live, this earth,
And life's itself a grand and glorious thing.
I love to live. Each coming day doth bring
Enough of the supremest, rarest joy,
To compensate for all its direst ills,
And leave enough beside to make God kind

And life a blessing. I would live, and take
The mingled cup from out the hand of God,
And bless him for the mingling. God is good,
And earth is good, and good hearts throb, between,
In many human bosoms.

The Stranger. (*Near her, unobserved.*)
Strange words are those! And yet not very strange
For one so young and fair. The world would turn
Its sweetest side to her, its side of love,
Drawn by the magnet of her purity.
But let her walk along its ways until
A single spot of its corruption clings
Unto her mantle; then, when sneering words,
And withering scorn, and curdled friendships meet
Her every step, then will she say, with me,
It is a wretched world, covered from crown to foot
With cankered and corroding wounds, that taint
The atmosphere with poison and with death.
It is a weary, wretched thing to live!
O, God! why must we live? An eager plea
For death—eternal, resurrectionless,
And all-destroying death—has gone to thee
From many, many thousand human hearts
Crushed, broken 'neath the weight of life thy hand
Hath placed upon them. Canst thou not destroy

What thou hast made? take that which thou hast
 given?
And unto me bestow the boon of death?
 'T is said that God is just. It is not just
To give us that, without our free consent,
Which we can not return. God gave us life
Without our will: we woke, and found its coil
Around us, and in vain we strive to free
Us from its ever-tightening folds; we live,
Struggling with life, until, wearied at last,
Baffled at every turn, in wild despair
We cry to God to ravel out the web
Of our existence, and to draw the thread
Again within himself. But ever on
The shuttle flies as swiftly to and fro,
Inweaving blackness and despair for aye.
We live, and live. Death comes to beasts how blest.
How blest were I could it but come to man!
 O, Lethe! fit to be a stream of heaven!
How sweet to float upon thy waveless breast
Down to the everlasting silences,
Where not a song, or sigh, or any sound
Of life or being shall disturb for aye
The stillness, more intense than is the joy
Of heaven or agony of hell! Listen!

Victoria. (*Singing.*)

Joy! joy! joy!
There is joy for thee, O Earth!
The golden Morn,
Of beauty born,
With its amber dews
And changing hues,
With its tender skies,
Whose image lies
In the sparkling sea,
That exultantly
Lifts up its voice,
And cries, "Rejoice!"
With its song that floats
From a million throats,
With its bursting blooms
And rare perfumes—
All the glorious things
That the morning brings
On her quivering wings
Are a joy to thee, O Earth!

Joy! joy! joy!
Each sound is full of joy.
From the faintest sigh of the swelling leaves,
And the twitter of birds beneath the eaves,
And the laugh of the rill down the mountain side,
To the booming roar of the tossing tide;
From the tenderest trill to the deepest tone,
There's a gushing fullness of joy alone—
Of joy that is thine, O Earth!

Joy! joy! joy!
There is joy for thee, O Heart!
The life that fills
Thy veins, and thrills,
With quickening heat,
Each pulse's beat;
The power that dwells
Deep, deep below,
Like hidden wells
That silent flow,
But that upward spring
Like a mighty thing,
When a gushing thought
Into deed is wrought;
The aims that rise
Beyond the skies;
The love that lies
Like a peaceful sea,
Whose waters lave,
With songful wave,
Immensity;
Each glorious thing
That Life doth bring
On her glancing wing,
Is a joy to thee, O Heart!

Joy! joy! joy!
O, life is full of joy!
And 'mid the sounds that swell on high
From the lips of Earth, triumphantly,
There blends for aye a low refrain,

A softer sound, a sweeter strain;
'T is the voice of Life, and its thrilling tone
Sings the gushing song of joy alone—
Of joy that is thine, O Heart!

How lovely is the scene in yonder dell,
As opened from this winding path! How fit
To be the home of her whose cottage stands
Within that quiet nook, behind the trees,
Where evermore the babble of the brook
Fills every room with sweetly-murmuring sounds,
So like a lullaby, it seems the place
For weary hearts that seek for peace and rest;
And that hers is a weary heart I feel.
Beneath the cheerfulness that crowns her brow,
And wreathes in smiles about her quiet lips
Whene'er they open to her voice, that thrills
One like the notes of some Æolian harp,
There sits a pensive sadness, like the dusk
Of Eve that, wedded to the parting Day,
Brings forth the twilight hour. She seems like one
Whose broken heart by Gilead's balm was healed.
It is the light of heavenly faith, not hope
Of earthly joy, that so illumes her face;
And it is love, as broad as human kind,
And charity for every human fault,

That adds that graciousness unto her mien
That wins so on the hearts of all.
But ah!
How sweet these violets in the meadow-grass!
I 'll gather them for her; their fragrant breath
To her shall whisper of the verdant fields
She loves so well, and win for me a smile.

SCENE III.

WITHIN THE COTTAGE OF LONESOME DELL. HERTHA, AN INVALID, ATTENDED BY HER MOTHER.

Mother. Thy heart is sad, my daughter.
Hertha. Very sad.
Mother. And dost thou think thy mother's heart is full
At last—so full that it can bear no more?
Hertha. Nay, mother; but I fear sometimes 't will break
Beneath the cross thy love doth bear for me.
Mother. A heavier cross than thine was borne, my love,
Both for thy sake and mine, by sinlessness,
Up Calvary's steep ascent; 't is meet we bear
Our little cross for him; if needs must be
We die upon it, Paradise will seem
More fair as entered by the path he trod—
The path of suffering through love.
Hertha. But ah!
If I might clasp her to my yearning heart

One blissful moment as my child, and hear
Her dear voice call me "Mother," it doth seem
I then could die content. But O, to think
That other grave should evermore receive
Her pious care, while that which hides the breast
Where first her head was pillowed lies unsown,
Unloved, as holding alien dust.
These years,
Since first I learned that holy lesson sweet
Of reconciliation to my lot,
I 've tried to act the teacher's humble part,
While all the mother throbbed within; and when,
As oft, her happy face has turned to mine,
With look of trusting confidence and love,
The swift-inflowing tide has almost cast
Me at her feet, with the confession strange,
A humble suppliant for her grace. But love
Hath checked the words it fain would speak. My lips
Could not reveal the tale, whose wretchedness
Would blight the bursting blossoms of her life
With mildew, e'en as it has mine; and still
She comes and goes, touches my trembling hand,
Kisses my cheek with all the grave respect
Due to my office, dreamless 't is her right,

By nature's law, to lie upon my breast,
And tell her little tale of hope and fear.
Sometimes I almost think within her heart
She holds unwittingly a daughter's love
For me.
I do believe there is a power
That binds the soul unto its kindred own—
A sweet affinity, like that which draws
The sundered particles to form a whole
That will reveal our true relationship
Erelong. But will she love me then? O God!
I trust thy hand to ravel out this web
Of thine own weaving, mystery, and pain.
I trust thee; for I know thy kindness still.

Mother. Mysterious are his dealings with thee, child.
Painful his kind corrections seem; but still
His blessing hath been thine. His hand hath kept
Her feet in paths of virtue and of peace,
And made her presence blest through all these years
To those upon whose care you, fainting, cast
The little, helpless babe. It was his hand
That led you there—in leading gave a home
Unto a storm-cast nestling, brought a joy
Too deep for earth unto a darkened soul.

It is a Providence of tenderest love
That guides the feet of man. O, trust Him still!

Hertha. I trust him, mother, leaning on his staff
Of strength, which is my only safe support.
Some reeds that grew along the streams of earth
I plucked to lean upon, they seemed so tall
And fair: they broke beneath my hand, and left
My choice but this, that seemed so gnarled and old.
I grasped it, and it bore my weary weight
O'er the rough path of sorrow cold and drear;
And now it beareth almond blooms most sweet,
And I am grateful and content, though oft
My mother-heart will pine for one fond look
Of recognition from my child.
But wait,
My heart! The dial-plate of God's own time
May point the hour of consummated hope
Before he calls thee hence, when thou shalt know
A mother's thrilling joy. A wife's? alas!

Mother, last night I dreamed of him. He came
And spake my name beneath the casement there.
"Hertha, my wife!" he said. Eager I flew
Along the path; he met me, and embraced
Most tenderly, then placed within my arms
An infant, sleeping as she slept that time,

And softly said, "Our little babe, sweet wife!"
In that old, tender way that won my heart;
And then I said, "It is a dream—a dream!
I shall awake erelong to sadder tears."
"Thou hast been dreaming, love, these years," he said;
"But this is not a dream."

O mother, say!
Which is delusion—which is true? the grief
Of a deserted heart, or the sweet joy
Of love, with love repaid? Perhaps 't is true
I have but only dreamed; and now she lies
In yonder room in sleeping innocence,
And will awake erelong to claim my care,
And chase the sad impressment from my heart.

Mother. Be calm, my child. 'T is wildness thus to talk.
Recline upon this couch, and I will bathe
The fever from thy brow till thou shalt sleep.
Ah, listen! There's a step.

Hertha. 'T is she! I know
The soft fall of her foot. Upon my ear
'T is like the music of the Summer rain
That falls on flowers.

O, panting heart, be still! (*Enter Victoria.*)

Dear child, then thou hast not forgot the days
In yonder school-room spent so happily?
Victoria. Forgot? with such a sweet remembrancer
As the dear face whose all-pervading smile
Has set them in the light of such a grace?
Hertha. And dost thou love me, then?
Victoria. I love thee? Yea;
With the same love, it seems, I should have borne
My own sweet mother had she lived until
My soul had caught the holy art from her.
And is not this love's fittest offering?
'T is meet that I should gather flowers for her
Who taught me first how beautiful they are.
Hertha. Thanks for thy flowers; their breath is very sweet.
I love the violet; all women do—
All who have suffered much, or who have loved.
Nature's most pure evangelists are they,
Writing the holy passion of her heart
In that soft hue, the type of constancy
O'er all the vale.
The fittest epitaph
A loving hand can write above a tomb,
The sweetest symbol for a bridal wreath,

Are these meek violets. My faith in God
Grows stronger in their presence, and my love
For man. I think the Savior must have worn
Them on his breast, and often sighed to see
The language of these gentle ministers
Of his so little understood by man.
Is not the air balmy and soft to-day?

Victoria. Most fresh and clear, inspiring as new wine.

Hertha. Mother, I think I should find cheerfulness
Where falls the blessed sunlight, softly, round
The shadow of that group of elms beside
The brook; and cheerfulness is health to me.
Pray bear my chair into the shade a space,
Just far enough so I can lay my hand
Out in the sunshine. 'T is the robe of God:
A healing power will flow into my soul
If I but touch its hem. O, blessed light!
There was a time it seemed to mock my life,
And when for blindness I did almost pray,
It hurt my heart so with its look of joy.
But that has passed; and now I know the sun
Hath need to wear no more the garb of woe
For human sorrow, since that golden dawn
When it arose and found the world redeemed.

Victoria. I know a little song I love to sing
In early Summer morns; I 'll sing to thee.

(*Sings.*) It is morning. The feet of the sunshine,
Still wet from the river of Dews,
Glide gleefully over the uplands,
So fair in the Summer-time hues.

And the sweet-chiming voices of breezes
That herald the lovely envoy
Are chanting, "How fair on the mountains
The feet of the bringer of joy!"

And my glad spirit echoes the music
Thanking God that the sunshine was born—
Thanking God for the wonderful glory
That crowneth and mantleth the morn.

Hertha. A happy song, and very sweetly sung.
Victoria. I love to sing. My heart seems like a well
Of happiness, and song the power that lifts
It, like a fountain, to the throne of God.
Hertha. A blessed gift is that of song. It seals
Our kinship to the angelhood. I sang
My girlhood through; but I awoke one morn
With all the music frozen in my heart,
And I shall sing no more until I learn
The new song of the blest, in Paradise.

Victoria. And hath so drear a Winter fallen on
The Summer of thy life, that not a bird—
A single snow-bird—there is left to wake,
With its sweet chirp amid the leafless boughs,
A dream of Spring?

Hertha. Ah yes! No song of earth,
No dream of earthly Spring, can cheer again
The coldness of this Winter reign. But yet
It is not drear: the sun shines o'er the snow,
And Faith hath hung her sweet Æolian harp
Within the window, and the chillest winds
Wake softest music in my silent heart.

Victoria. I think there is a story of thy life
That I should love to know.

Hertha. Not yet—not yet.—
O, eager heart—O, whirling brain, be still! (*Aside.*)

Victoria. Forgive, forgive the blind request I made.
I would not cause thy heart a moment's pain.
O, that I could but bear thy grief, and give
Thee rest, instead!

Hertha. God shield thy heart, dear child!
I can not tell my story to thee now.
The time may come—but I have suffered much.
My heart had broken, but the hand of God

Encircled it with love, so that the blow
He kindly dealt upon his erring child
Was tempered to my strength to bear; and so
I am content. These sorrow-pangs are but
The birth-throes of a higher, nobler life
That shall be born in me, vital with love.
The joys of earth to me were all supreme.
O, I had dreamed of bliss, till castles long
And beautiful as wreathing river mists
Stood on the fairy landscape of my life.
A thousand fingered columns pointed up
To heaven, and held forever in their grasp
The sunlight, as my hand had held the flowers.
The air was full of perfume and of song;
The song was full of an ecstatic joy,
More blest than that which filled the blooming groves
Of Paradise. Above, there bent a sky
That seemed the type of heaven; and in the light
That fell from its high sun the peaceful scene
Transfigured lay unto my gaze, and like
The city out of sight, that blest the eyes
Of holy prophets as they looked upon
The mysteries of God.
I said in pride,
My heaven begins below. O, golden Earth!

I ask no sweeter life than thou hast given!
When suddenly I stood transformed with fear,
And wildly gazed as, with a motion slow
And like the upward lifting of a cloud,
The dear, entrancing scene had all dissolved
Into the distant heaven. Darkness around
Me fell, and I was wrung with agony
Of soul, while earth and heaven to chaos turned,
And were as though they had not been. Alone
I groped to find a way, when came a voice
That bade the light break forth. I turned, and lo!
Another world of more substantial mold,
A city with foundations, sprung to life.
My feet were guided in the ways of peace,
And so I am content to wait my time—
To tread the path, though thorny it may be,
That leads to joys eternal and secure.
But I have found a gentle comforter
In Nature, and a sweet diversion from
My grief in contemplation of her moods.
To him who loves to tread her sacred courts,
Each expiration of whose breath ascends
In praise with that of swinging flowers, offerings
Of incense sweet, acceptable to God,
The firm, pure throbbings of whose heart are timed

Unto the loving pulses of her own—
To him she doth unfold her secret stores,
Reveal the rarest pages of her book
Of hidden revelations, deep and grand,
And measures to his soul the fullness of
A joy that she alone could give. And when
His feet shall pause at last before the vail
That hides the inner temple from his view—
When strains of that new song that 's sung within
Float out in triumph, blending with the low,
Retreating notes of the terrestrial choir—
Her hand shall gently part the shadowy vail,
And guide his trembling, unclad feet into
The Holiest of Holies, where, between
The bending cherubim, Shekinah dwells,
Before the unvailed glory of whose face
The eye shall gather newer light, the heart
Shall throb with inspiration of a life
It never felt before, as far above
The groveling, sinful life of earth as is
The thought of God above the thought of man—
Upon whose wings of tireless energy
It shall mount up, with song and shout of joy,
Until he stands upon the holy hill,
White-robed, for evermore a priest of God!

Mother. Thy cheek is flushed, as if with weariness.

Hertha. Nay; 't is the flush of inspiration from
The heart of God, that quivers in these leaves,
And pulses in the waves that beat upon
The shore. Mother, I feel Him very near,
E'en as I feel thy presence. I am blest!

Mother. But yield thou to thy mother's judgment, love,
And let us lead thee to thy room. Thy couch
Shall stand the window 'neath that overlooks
The meadow and the brook, and thou shalt rest.

Hertha. Thy wish is law, dear mother. I am still
Thy child, in duty still obedient. (*They lead her in.*)

Victoria. I am reminded of my duteous cares.
I left my father sleeping; he will need
My hand to guide him in his evening walk;
So I will crave thy blessing, and depart.

Hertha. My blessing follows thee, dear child; my prayers
Environ all thy ways. God keep thy steps!
Come soon again; the gladness of thy voice
Doth cheer my heart, and half beguile my lips
Into a song concerting with thine own.
Yon instrument is voiceless all these days.

I still would teach thee while my strength remains,
If thou shouldst please: so with my finer art
Repay thee for the gladness thou dost bring.

Victoria. The rarest pleasure 'tis to learn of thee,
And, nothing loth, gladly I will renew
Companionship with music and with thee.

SCENE IV.

BY THE LAKE. ERNEST AND VICTORIA.

Ernest. This old, familiar seat—how dear it grows
With each declining day! Two score of years
Have passed since that bright Summer-time when we—
My brother Thorn and I—that sapling vine
Twisted into a chair for forms we loved.
Ah! how, each coming Spring, we gladly hailed
The first mild eve, when we could lead the way
With bounding feet, followed, with slower steps,
By those for whom our little toil was spent!
Sweet mother! honored sire! Long since they slept.
Thank Heaven! it was before the day he fell
Whose fall had crushed the hearts that went to rest
So sweetly in our arms, with not a dream
Of a dishonored name. They sleep in peace.
But thou, my gentle brother, where art thou?
My eyes have darkened since they saw thy face;
My head has whitened since I have received

Assurance that thou still rememberest me.
Ah! how I loved thee! How I love thee still,
God, who hath known my midnight prayers and tears,
Alone can tell. I pray his grace to keep
Thy feet where'er they roam, if still they tread
The ways of earth! But thou hast found ere this,
I think, thy grave somewhere beneath the heavens,
Thy home, I trust, above.
But all are gone!
And the sweet bride, whose face was the last thing
My eyes e'er looked upon; and I am left,
A poor old man, alone and blind.

Victoria. Nay, nay—
Not left alone, my father; here am I.

Ernest. True, child; and I am blest in thee. My eyes,
My staff, my sweet companion, thou hast been
These many years, e'en since the Autumn day
When Ruth did find thee in the garden path.

Victoria. Since Ruth did find me?
Am I not thy child?
Was not my mother she whose grave within
Yon dell I've wreathed with flowers each Spring since first

You led me there a toddling child? O speak,
And tell me, father, that I am thy child!

Ernest. My child thou art by every tie but that
Of Nature. Nay, love, do not tremble so;
But sit thee down beside me here, and list
The little tale I have to tell, that thou
Art old enough to hear; that is thy right.
'T was eighteen years ago this Autumn-time—
A weary day: all days were weary then.
Each morn I sadly counted o'er the days
Since I had seen the sun; each eve, the nights
Since that in which she died—the day and night
Which cut my life in two, from which, like blood
From out a severed vein, there flowed the joy.
I had been mourning all the day; my heart
Seemed cold with grief. Poor Ruth had tried in vain
All arts of comforting, until, at last,
Wearied, she walked into the field to cheer
Her heart, so saddened at the sight of me.
Not long she tarried, when along the path
I heard her stepping quickly, as in haste,
As I had never known before. She came,
And, in a voice that quivered like the sound
Swept from the slackened strings of some old harp,
Exclaimed, "O, master, it is very strange!

But as I walked along the garden path
I found, close by the yellow jessamine
Your mother loved, a little sleeping babe."
"A sleeping babe!" with eagerness I cried,
With a strange yearning in my heart; "a babe!
Pray give it me." She placed you in my arms,
And said, in her so trusting, childlike way,
"Truly, the Lord hath sent it. You have wished,
Full many times, your wife had left a child:
The Lord hath heard, and lo! thy field
Brings forth thy soul's desire, and Ruth hath gleaned
For thee."
I took the little form, and pressed
It to my heart; I gently passed my hand
The tiny features o'er, to trace their mold;
I felt the broad, smooth brow, the silken curls
That clustered round its arch, the fringèd lids
That opened at my touch, with motion like
The unfolding of a flower, the little hand
That, folded, lay beneath the swelling cheek,
Whose fingers quickly fixed their clasp on mine.
Dreaming I sat, and wondering, till at last
There came a frightened cry. I hushed it with
A lullaby, who had not sung for years.
I think I had not been so near to heaven

Since first I lay, just such a helpless babe,
Within my mother's arms. But then there came
A thought: it is not mine. A thrill of pain
Passed through my frame; I clasped thee closer
still—
So close that thou didst cry from pain. Ruth came
And took thee from my arms, to soothe with arts
That women understand; and then I asked
What I had feared to ask, or know, till then,
"Who brought the child? and will they not return
To give it guardianship erelong? No heart
Could cast away a jewel rare as this."
"I only saw a footprint in the sand,"
Old Ruth replied, "a small foot like a girl's.
It is, mayhap, the old, sad tale of love,
And sin, and shame, that seeks to hide itself
Within the quiet of this still retreat.
The wee, sweet darling! Let us take the gift
As sent of God, for comfort and for hope,
Until, at least, some one with better right
Shall take her from our care." And it was so.
Old Ruth found beating in her maiden breast
A mother's tender heart. A mother's care
She gave through all these years with faithful love.
And I? My life fresh blossomed in thy smile;

My arms were thy sole cradle. Rocking thee,
I sat for hours, and felt my manhood grow
From out the darkness of despair into
The calm, sweet light of hope. I won thee to
Thy slumbers with the songs my mother sang
In my own childhood's happy days; and song
Brought cheerfulness. There is no antidote
So sure as song for that most subtile poison
Of the soul, a brooding melancholy;
And I began to laugh, like other men,
The ringing, hearty laugh of health and hope.
And thus, in calm content and healthful joy,
That gathered freshness from each rosy dawn
And sweeter sleep from every waxing moon,
Passed on the days and months, that grew to years,
And brought no claimant for our charge, no sign
Of aught that could connect thee with the world
Beyond our quiet cot, until, one day,
When thou hadst grown a laughing, romping girl,
Some six years old, you wandered to the grove
Beyond the garden, after wildwood flowers.
You had been gone full long, when Ruth came in,
In haste, and asked for you. She feared some ill
Had come to you, she said; for she had seen
Those footprints on the sand that marked the day

When first you came. "The child is gone!" she said,
And wept as though she mourned the dead. My heart
Grew faint, then almost wild; I quite forgot
I could not see, and hasted o'er the path,
And called your name aloud. You came at last,
And sprang into my arms, your apron full
Of flowers. Your happy lips in childish prattle
Answered to my chiding with the tale
Of one—a pretty lady, as you said—
Who came and called you forth, and talked with you.

Victoria. Ah, now I do remember well the time.
She kissed me o'er and o'er again, and wept;
But I had never thought it strange till now.
I have a dim remembrance of her face:
It oft hath floated through my happy dreams,
With mien of those who walk in Paradise;
And I have always thought it was the face
Of her above whose grave we 've blent our tears.

Ernest. For thirty years the grass hath grown, my child,
Upon that grave.

Victoria. I never thought to ask
Or know before.

Ernest. I wished thou shouldst not know,
Until thy story might be safely told.

Victoria. Who was this lady, father? Can it be
She was my mother?

Ernest. Thou dost know, my love,
As well as I. I have no more to tell
That is not known to thee. From thence thy days
Passed on like other girls', with tasks at home,
That Ruth, with mother's thoughtfulness, hath placed
Before thy hand, against thy womanhood—
Duties at school and recreations sweet.
But, unlike others, hath thy mission been
To lift the darkness from a soul like mine,
And with the brightness of thy presence, dear,
O'ershine a spirit's night.
The day may come
That shall reveal this mystery of thy life;
Till then thou art my child, my precious child,
And I thy fond old sire.
There, do not weep;
Or lay thy head here on my breast; 't will be
The rock on which thy grief shall beat, and flow
Back to the peaceful sea.

Victoria. I do not think
'T is grief that makes me weep; it is a strange,
Oppressive sense of isolation from
My kin; uncertainty, like that of one
Without identity; an atom torn
From every kindred particle; a link
Cut from the generations whence I sprung,
And left to rust beside the way.

Ernest. Nay, nay;
A link that God upon the anvil of
His love hath welded to a chain where it
Was needed more. Lie thou within his hand
Till he bestow the luster that reflects
The glory of his face divine.

Victoria. How strange!
And all my life hath been so full of joy!
I ne'er had dreamed so sad a fate as this
Could find a sacrifice in me. But now
I think some fruits must fall from every tree.

Ernest. Some fruit must fall that what is left may be
More excellent; and so in the rough wind
'T is kind to shake the overladen boughs
That else had ripened but imperfect fruits,
Or from the fount had overflowed, and left

The roots withered, famished with thirst, to
brave
The Winter's racking storms. Be patient, then;
Our ever-faithful Husbandman doth care
For all the branches of his vine; no sprig
Shall wither from neglect, or be plucked off
By chance or wantonness. Trust thou in Him:
The future years shall yet reveal to thee
The wisdom that disposed thy lot in life.

Victoria. Father, I can but trust the loving
Christ.
But O, I fain would always be thy child
As now! O, take me in thine arms, and say
I am thy precious child, thy blessing still,
As thou so lovingly hast told me oft.
I feel so cold, as though the north-wind blew
Athwart my heart!

O, that my mother's hand
Should cast my helpless, guileless infancy
From the protection of her breast, unloved!
Mother! mother! I thought thou wert in heaven.
The name that I have whispered to the stars,
And wrought in wreaths of sweetest flowers, each
Spring,
Upon yon grave, shall mock my love for aye.

Ernest. There, there! I'll sing to thee as I have done
To soothe thy childish griefs. There is a song
My mother sang, when disappointment's hand
Had set her heart a-chiming to its tune,
That is most sweet and comforting. I'll sing:

One by one they fall, the blossoms
  That perfumed the Spring-time air.
Where they bloomed swing ripened clusters,
  Globes of juices, bland and rare.

O, the boughs bend 'neath the burden
  That shall make our store complete;
And we bless the wind that scattered
  All the blossoms at our feet.

One by one they fall, lamented,
  Hopes we cherished all our Spring;
But upon the Summer branches
  Richer joys begin to swing.

They shall ripen, full and golden,
  Pleasures sweet and deeds sublime,
And we'll bless the storms that scattered
  Flowers, to give a fruitful prime.

Of my old harp the strings are growing slack
And tuneless; but there soon will come a day
When, strung anew, its notes shall float upon

A thousand echoes o'er the mount of God,
Eternal love the burden of its song.
  Now, go thou to thy room, and talk with God.
Lay thou thy head upon his hand, and sleep,
And peace, that water-lily pure and sweet,
Shall open on this river of thy tears
Its snowy petals to the morning light.

SCENE V.

CLEONE AND VICTORIA BY THE LAKE.

Cleone. The lake is motionless. The waters lie
Beneath the full-orbed moon, as pale as death,
Save near the western shore, where lingers yet
The roseate flush of life, like that which tints
The cheek of childhood in its balmy sleep,
Revealing the yet beating heart beneath
The mask of death. There is not wave enough
To float that rose-leaf scattered from thy hand.
I had not thought thou couldst despoil a flower.

Victoria. 'T was but a leaf some worm had spoiled before.
I plucked it off because it blotted so
The perfectness of this sweet rose. Ah me!

Cleone. Wherefore that sigh, beloved? 'T were worth far more
Than one poor, blighted leaf.

Victoria. Ah, Cleone, nay.
God made the leaf that but a worm destroyed.

But come; I 'll take this oar and measure strokes
With thee.

Cleone. This tiny skiff I chose because
It seems so light and airy in its form
That it might be to us, on this calm sea,
Like Wordsworth's crescent moon for speed and
grace.
How smooth and noiseless part the waters from
Our cleaving prow, to spread in ripples out,
And wake a murmur on the silent shore!
The pathway of our dipping oars is traced
In dimples like to those that come with smiles.
With what a bold relief each shadowed shape
Of curving shore, of swelling hill, and tree,
And overreaching branch or vine is thrown
Upon the whiteness of this silvered plain!
Yon elm-tree and that blackened, shivered stub,
From which those long festoons of ivy swing
In generous wreaths, to hide his nakedness,
Growing upon the point of Willhelm's Cape,
So like the shadows seem unto the real
That they appear but one, branching alike
Beneath the waters and above.

I 've seen
The Maggiore, when it lay beneath

Italia's sweetest sky—a poet's dream—
And fair Geneva in its glacier bed,
A liquid crescent, sweetly smiling back
Unto its sister Moon; Loch Lomond wild,
With giant hills and crags, encircled round;
Each rare in its peculiar loveliness;
But I have ne'er beheld a scene more fair
Than this. The rocky promontory bald,
The wooded hill and gently-sloping shore,
That spreads its verdure for the waves to tread—
These, with their wreathing curves, fondly embrace
Our own sweet Minnetonka's sweeping bays.

Victoria. Ah! whence that shaft of light that shot, just now,
Athwart our prow—just flashed, then disappeared?

Cleone. 'T was from the torch upon some fishing skiff.
Ah! there it streams from out those shadowed depths,
A liquid vein of fire across the waves.
They little deem how their small fagot torch
Does glorify the calm face of the lake,
As gliding out and in, so spirit-like,
Among the shadows of the shore, it seems

Some wandering star that thought this quiet sea
Might be its native heaven.
List! how that strain
Of happy music thrills this dreamy air!
Music upon the waters! How its voice
Grows tender singing to the moonlit waves!
We 'll rest upon our oars, and heed the song.

SONG.

O, lightly lift the dipping oar,
And swiftly, swiftly glide,
While gladly beats each happy heart,
Across the peaceful tide.
Lightly row, lightly row;
For our hearts are light, you know;
And our song shall speed along
Those who lift the oars, you know;
Maiden song, speed along
Those who lift the oars, you know.

O, calmly flow the peaceful waves
Upon the Summer sea,
And starlight on its pulsing breast
Is pillowed tenderly.
Lightly row, lightly row,
In the starlight's tender glow;
And our song shall speed along
Those who lift the oars, you know;
Maiden song shall speed along
Those who lift the oars, you know.

O, oarsmen, life is but a sea,
  A calm, sweet Summer sea,
And lovelight on its pulsing breast
  Is pillowed tenderly.
Then lightly, lightly row,
In the lovelight's tender glow;
  And our song shall speed along
Those who lift the oars, you know;
  Maiden song, speed along
Those who lift the oars, you know.

A crew of merry voyagers are they
Who gayly sang that tender melody,
Nor dreamed its holy meaning, as you thumbed
One day your harp-strings, while your mind was far
From the sweet tune that from your fingers fell,
Won by the touch it well had learned to know.
That thoughtless chime did fill my eyes with tears,
And their sweet song is echoed in our hearts—
In thine and mine, my own beloved, my bride.
Victoria. Cleone! Cleone! my heart will break!
Cleone. Will break?
Victoria. Would break, but that I know that God is good,
And that his providence doth mark our ways
With mercy and with loving-kindness still.
I can not wed thee, Cleone—can not link

My blighted life with thine. I, without name
Or parentage, an offcast, foundling child,
And thou so honored, so beloved by all.

Cleone. But thou art mine, Victoria—art mine,
Mine by the vows thy lips did plight to me,
And naught but God our lives shall sever now.
Nay, do not speak—I know thy story well.
He whom thou call'st thy father told it me,
So thoughtful of thy life-long happiness,
Once, when I asked thee at his faithful hand.
"Take her," he said, "the blind man's light and joy;
For I am passing from her guiding hand,
And she, my little, fragile jessamine,
Will need a far more firm support than mine
When life shall bring its Winter wind and storm.
Take her, and guard with love's most gentle care,
And she will bless thy heart as she has mine."
Wilt thou deny my hand its holy task?
Wilt bring to naught his tender prophecy?
Thou answerest not; then hast thou never loved.

Victoria. O Love! next sweetest, holiest name to Christ!
How it hath floated up and down my soul,
Set to the music of life's grandest tune

Of almost heavenly joy, thou canst not know.
Did I but love thee less, no agony
Like this had strung my heart. As wife alone
The happy years might bring forgetfulness;
But ah! 't were sin to blight another life,
Offspringing from my own, with such a stain
Of darkness and of shame. I do not know
What fruits upon my tree ancestral grew;
What passions may be latent in my veins;
What slow-consuming fires of dire disease
May smolder 'neath this outward bloom of health;
And, Cleone, though my maiden cheek may blush,
I must obey my woman's heart, and speak.
I can not cloud the name thy children fair
With honor must perpetuate to thee.
May God forgive me that I stole thy love,
To thrust it, like a dagger, to thy heart
At last, so barbed with woe! Wilt thou forgive?

Cleone. And dóst thou love me, then, Victoria?

Victoria. I love thee, Cleone? As the eye doth love
The dawning day.

Cleone. Then shalt thou yet be mine.
The time must come that will remove thy fears,
And give thine honest heart the right to wed.
We 'll trust in God, and lovers be till then.

SCENE VI.

ERNEST SITTING IN THE DOOR. RUTH ABOUT THE FLOWER-PLATS.

Ernest. How thrive your children of the garden, Ruth?

Ruth. Most finely, master, as the girls and boys
Have learned full well: they love my pretty flowers.
I have to make a wreath or shoulder-knot
For every romping girl the village through,
And nosegays for the boyish lovers too,
With which they win these maiden, bashful smiles.
But then they pay me well with happy talk,
And sparkling look, and many a dewy kiss,
And now and then some treasure from the woods
That I have grown at last too old to search.
And, then, I think my heart doth younger grow
Beneath the touch of childhood and of flowers.
Fair Mary Earle, the bride of yester-eve,
Wore half-blown roses from this damask-tree,
Twined with blue violets, amid her curls;
And these bright stars of Bethlehem were cast

By many hands upon the pall that lay
So dark above the gentle Bertie Gray;
And but this eve a stranger, pale and wan,
Leaned on the gate, and asked me for a spray
Of this Adonis, and he looked so sad
I could but bind a daisy to its stem,
That it might whisper patience to his heart.
He looked e'en thankful as he went his way.

Ernest. These little blossoms, then, are ministers
Of peace and comfort in thy hands, and speak
A language varied to the ears of men.

Ruth. Ay; and it gives me comfort, as I prune,
And dig, and train the wanton boughs; and oft
I think if I may weave a few fair flowers
Into the borders of my life, so coarse
With toil and care, it will appear, at last,
More beautiful, more fit to wear unto
The marriage of the Lamb.

Ernest. Thy life, good Ruth,
Is wrought of finer tissues than you deem.
But ah! I miss my little girl to-night.
Is the lake smooth? Come, let me take your hand,
And we will go and wait them on the beach.
Hark! there 's a sound of rushing waves I hear.

'T is rough beyond the bay; the wind is high.
Dost thou not hear?

Ruth. Ay; and the skiff is gone,
The frailest boat of all. So calm it seemed,
They had no thought of fear.

Ernest. O God! O God!

SCENE VII.

THE STRANGER ON THE LAKE SHORE.

Stranger. Ah, Minnetonka, wild and beautiful!
How changed! An hour ago thou wert as calm
As though a breath had never marred thy brow,
Smiling so sweetly to the smiling moon;
Now, fierce with rushing waves and dashing foam,
Dost fling her wild, distorted image back
Upon a thousand mad, impetuous hands,
As if some secret anger vexed thy depths.
Is it because my shadow fell athwart
Thy waters? All the world with loathing looks
On me, as do the eyes of Heaven; and yet
I thought the woman at the gate did look
Most kindly in my face, and that wee flower
Did seem so sweet a gift, my heart hath felt
Not quite so lonely, quite so sinful, since.
If there might be a hope! But no—ah no!
All love for me hath withered from the world;
For me there blooms no love in heaven. Alone
I am, an alien from the universe.

She lives in the old cot, the little maid
Whom I have met, who seems so full of joy.
Why yearns my heart so to that girlish form?
Her face I have not seen: it must be fair.
Her voice seems like familiar melody,
And thrills me with emotion strange and sad.
I think I 'll go some day—I 'll make excuse,
And cross the dear old threshold once again,
And hear the fate of those who dwelt with me
Within those walls, from her.
How wild the waves
Are panting on the beach, as though their strife
To mock the rage of ocean's boiling surf
Had wearied them, until they sink at last,
With smothered laughter, on the shell-strewn shore!
'T is strange the waves should seem to me to laugh;
But there 's a witchery in the scene to-night
That doth e'en tempt my heart to cheerfulness.
If I might bind one human soul to mine
By gratitude, if not by holy love—
Could I forget those blotted, weary years,
I think I might be e'en a man again.
But O, my gentle wife, my guileless child!
My soul must expiate its sin to you
With agony immortal as its life!

But ah! what floating form is that I see
Just rounding Stony Point? (*Runs down the beach.*)
A skiff! a skiff!
It must be dashed upon those rugged rocks,
Should the rough waves not overwhelm before.
How wildly it is tossed! So frail a thing,
Lured forth by the deceitful loveliness
That on the waters sat at eventide!
Ah! that a human life should be the stake
Of such unequal strife! God save their souls!
Another surf like that and she must sink!
It comes! it comes! the cruel, heartless sea!

A Woman's Voice. O, save us! save!

Stranger. That voice! 'T is she! 't is she!
I'd know it 'mid a thousand roaring seas.
She must be saved! It is a manly arm
That holds her in those madly-whirling waves;
But he must fail erelong. I'll to his aid.
(*Plunges into the water.*)

SCENE VIII.

ERNEST AND RUTH ON THE SHORE.

Ruth. Pray, master, let me lead thee in; the air
Is cool, at this late hour, for thee to bear.
Ernest. Nay; I will sit here till the waves shall
float
Her to the shore; then I will fold her form
Close to my breast again, and die.
Ruth. Not so;
Dear master, speak not so. They may have found
Some place of safety from the gale, or shore
Where they might wait until the storm is passed.
The lake is narrow, and there 's many a bay,
So sheltered that its waters must be calm—
As calm as this. But we must trust in Him
Whose breath of love did wake the sleeping waves.
I sent the gardener, on the fleetest horse,
To search the shores on which these seas do break,
And in the brightness of this fullest moon
Naught will escape his eye. He will return
Erelong, I trust, with comfort for our hearts.

Hark! there 's a sound of dashing hoofs I hear,
And I do think they have a ring of joy.

Gardener. (*Shouting to them.*) They 're safe! all safe!

Ernest. (*Kneeling.*) O God, accept my praise!
Forgive the heart that erst did doubt thy love.

Gardener. (*Approaching.*) I met——

Ruth. Speak not! He prays—the poor old man!
I thought his heart would break.

Ernest. Speak on! speak on!

Gardener. I met them just beyond the bridge that spans
The straits. Lame Willie brings them in his coach.
I knew your anguish, sir, and hasted back
With my brief message, that it might console
Until you hear the story at their lips.
List! I do hear the rumbling of the wheels,
And I will lead you in. Good Ruth hath gone,
With thoughtful care and her most skillful hands,
To set all things in order for their need,
For comfort and for health. (*They enter.*)
Here is your chair. (*Enter Cleone.*)

Cleone. Kind Roger, lend in aid thy sturdy hand. (*They leave the room.*)

Ernest. (*Alone.*) O, dread suspense! My heart is sick with fear.

Why called he thus for help? She must be dead,
And still they fear to tell it me. O God!
I am a poor old man, alone and blind:
Have pity on me, tender heart of love!
O, leave me not to find my grave alone!

(*Enter Victoria and Ruth.*)

Victoria. Father!

Ernest. My child! my child! then thou art here?

Victoria. Here, father, rescued from the whelming waves.
The gale so suddenly arose that we,
All unprepared, could reach no harbor calm.
We tried to stem the sea, but it was vain.
At last, with broken oars and sinking boat,
We closely clasped each other's hands, and prayed.
The moon and stars looked coldly from above
In their eternal calm; the waves beneath
More cold did seem in their wild restlessness.
I thought of thee, and wept and prayed again;
And then I thought of heaven, that country fair,
And said, "These are but Jordan's waves to us;
Yonder our Canaan lies." My soul grew calm
At this, as though it lay God's hand within.
We silent sat, and waited for the wave
That should infold us like a winding-sheet,

While we should sleep upon our shell-strewn bed.
It came, at last we thought. The boat was full;
It sank, and sank. We hung amid the waves
One little breath, then over us they rolled.
I thought the world was drowned; 't was very cold.
But then a strong arm that I thought was God's,
(So turns the soul to him in time of fear,)
Upheld me, and a brave voice said, "Courage!
There 's aid at hand!" I looked across the waste
Of swiftly-rushing waters to the shore,
And there was one who ran in haste. I cried,
"O, save us!' for the thought of life was sweet
E'en in the midst of death. He quickly plunged
Into the waters, grappled with the waves
That strove to hurl him backward on the strand,
And met us just as Cleone well-nigh sank,
Exhausted by my weight. They joined their strength,
And so at length the shore was gained. But he
Whose brave, strong arm had brought so timely aid
Sank breathless on the sand; and then we saw
That he was old. White as the ocean's foam
The beard that floated o'er his pulseless breast,
And pallid as the moon his face, and thin.
Cleone forgot his weariness, and ran

To Willie's cottage for sufficient aid.
They bore us thither, and in kindness gave
Us every needed care. The stranger seemed
So ill, and we so much his debtors are,
I could but bring him to our quiet home,
Where Ruth, the queen of nurses, kindly reigns.
And now he sleeps, I trust, upon the bed
She hath prepared for him, with Cleone near.

Ruth. He doth not sleep; his mind is wandering.
Roger hath gone for a physician now.

Ernest. Who is this stranger? where his home?

Ruth. 'T is he
To whom I gave those flowers this eventide—
A stranger to us all, and very ill.

Ernest. Give him most loving care. We owe him more
Than simple gratitude can ever pay.
And now we will commend him in our prayer,
So full of thankfulness and praise, to God.

SCENE IX.

ERNEST AND VICTORIA.

Ernest. How doth the stranger seem this morning, love?

Victoria. He sleepeth now just like a weary child.
His breath would scarcely sway a leaf, so faint
It floateth from his breast. His right hand lies
Where by his flowing beard 't is half concealed;
The other, with its bony fingers, clasps
The ever-faithful palm of good old Ruth.
He clings to her as to his mother; oft
His eye doth follow her with wistful look,
And rests so fond upon her answering gaze,
That it is pitiful to see. Poor man!

Ernest. Hath he returned to consciousness?

Victoria. Ah no!
There 's something very sad in his low talk
About his dear old home. 'T was near some lake.
He had a brother whom he fondly loved.
His mind hath dwelt upon their happy sports
With almost childish joy. It made me weep

To hear such playful words from lips that wore,
E'en then, a look so full of bitterness
That all his smiles did seem as sunshine set
Upon the edges of some dreary cloud.
I think he hath known sorrow, more than comes
To men within the common ways of life,
And sin, perhaps—though God must judge, not I—
For once he started from a fevered sleep,
And cried, in such a tone of agony,
"My wife! my wife! forgive!" Then sinking back,
He moaned, "My little child, forgive—forgive!"
I know, however great his sin hath been,
Could they but hear the pleading of that prayer,
The answer must descend, in loving tears
And kisses, on his brow. *(Enter Ruth.)*
What tidings, Ruth?

Ruth. He woke just now, and looked around, surprised;
Then calmly said, "Madam, have I been ill?"
"Yes, very ill," I said, "but now there 's hope."
And in my joy I did let fall a tear
Upon his face. He looked up wonderingly,
Then asked, "How did it happen? tell me, pray."
But I had scarce begun when he exclaimed,
"I do remember now. And are they safe?"

"Both safe and well," I answered, "and have watched
Beside thy bed these many days." He smiled,
Then asked, "Whose debtor am I for the care
So kindly given?" "Thou art no debtor, sir,"
I made reply, "but a most honored guest
At Ernest Raymond's cottage, the Retreat."
At this a look so strange came o'er his face:
He turned it to the wall, and wept. I said,
"Why do you weep? You must be very calm."
"O, I am as a little child," he sighed,
"And all doth seem so strange."
He soon grew calm,
And now he lieth still, with lips that move
As if in prayer. I stole away to tell
The change, so full of gladness for us all.

Ernest. I fain would meet this stranger: lead me in.
I may give comfort to him in his need,
Or teach him whence the sweetest comforts flow;
And I would tell him of my gratitude,
Acknowledging a debt I can not pay.

Ruth. I fear, dear master, he is yet too ill.

Ernest. I will be very quiet—let me go.
My daughter, lead the way.

Victoria. Here is the door. (*They enter.*)
Hush! he is sleeping. Seat thee in this chair
Till he awake.

Stranger. Nay, nay; I do not sleep.

Victoria. This is my father, Ernest Raymond, sir,
And he is blind.

Stranger. Is blind? Ah! here 's my hand.

Ernest. 'T is very thin. You have been ill, my friend.

Stranger. Yes, yes; I have been ill—and you most kind.

Ernest. Speak not of that. We owe a debt to you
Second alone to that we owe to God.
I came, this early moment, to express
My gratitude, as far as feeble words
Its depth of meaning to your ears can bear,
For the most timely aid that saved my life
From deeper darkness. Dark indeed my life,
Had the soft beaming of my evening star
In those wild waves gone out.
That God is good
I never more can doubt, his name be praised!
Have you, my friend, not learned from your own life
That lesson of his graciousness and love?

Stranger. My mother taught me at her knee to say
That God is love; but where it first begun
The lesson ended—turned long since the page
O'er which there lies full many a dark-stained leaf.

Ernest. You have known sorrow, then?

Stranger. Sorrow I knew
Beside my mother's grave. Then once I sinned,
And scorn hath dogged my steps around the world,
And now at last, self-seated in my heart,
Doth stare back on the staring world, the while
It gnaws upon the vitals of my soul.
Sorrow, and sin, and scorn—I know them well.

Ernest. Thy brain is fevered, friend; thou 'rt yet too ill
To dwell on thoughts like these. Trust thou in God,
And he will give thee comfort for thy woe,
Pardon for sin, and tenderest love for scorn.

Howe'er so bitter be the cup
  That stings thy shrinking lips,
Though deepest darkness o'er thy life
  Hath cast its sad eclipse;

Yet to the brim, before thine own,
  Were pressed the lips divine,
And holy feet did tread alone
  A way more dark than thine.

Once did this sinless sufferer pray,
  "Let this cup pass from me.
Nevertheless thy will be done:
  Father, I yield to thee."

Thy own heart's deepest woe he felt
  In lone Gethsemane;
And in his yearning, pitying love
  He wept and prayed for thee.

Then be not comfortless, but hear
  His pleading voice repeat,
"Come unto me, ye weary ones,
  For rest and comfort sweet."

I 'll leave thee now to rest. Be peace with thee!
Yet stay: thou hast some friend who hath a right
To hear of thy condition, and will feel
Most anxious for thy sake. 'T will please us well
To execute thy wish, but make it known.

Stranger. I have one brother, sir; but he forgot
Long since to love the one who brought disgrace
Upon the honored name he shares with me.
He will not care to hear.

Ernest. Not care to hear?
'T were sad indeed that thus estranged should grow
The feet whose early paths did lie so near.
I think if he hath yet a human heart,
He 'd e'en forgive and love thee still. Ah me!

'T would give me joy to clasp again the hand
Of my own gentle brother, long estranged.
I pray thee let me for thy brother do
This kindly office I would crave for me.

Victoria. Father, he weeps.

Ernest. Forgive, my friend; but still,
I pray, deny me not thy brother's name.

Stranger. 'T is Ernest Raymond. Love me, love me still!

Ernest. My brother? O, my Thornton, is it thou?

Victoria. He faints! he faints! His brow is very cold;
His breath was spent in that one cry for love.

SCENE X.

ERNEST AND THORNTON.

Thornton. This is the same old room in which they died.
The couch stood in that corner, and the stand
On which the open Bible lay beside.
It was a loss most sad when father died;
We needed still the guidance of his will.
But ah! when she, our gentle mother, passed
Beyond our reach, how drear and desolate
The world did seem! I do remember well
The time! 'T was sunset, and the slanting beam
Pierced through the woodbine o'er the window there,
And lay upon the floor in golden flakes,
'Mid shadowed leaves that wavered to and fro.
The waters of the lake were all ablaze
With such resplendent glory that it seemed
Most fitting she should say, as twice she did,
"The sea of glass! the sea of glass!" as though
The prophet's vision blessed her failing eyes.

That same old clock did time, with measured stroke,
Each second that so added to our woe,
Until at last its solemn bell did toll
The hour that found us motherless, alone.
How much it meant to me thou dost not know,
My senior by a half a score of years,
Always so strong and fearless, formed to lead,
And I so yielding, ever needing more
The firm, sure guidance of a loving hand.
Thy life, my brother, had its blighting, too:
The sudden night that fell upon thy day,
The loss so sad of wife, so well beloved!
But thou art blest in this one treasure left,
Thy daughter, perfect in her loveliness.
She hath our mother's face—the same low brow,
With such a wondrous breadth; the large, brown
eyes,
So filled with sweet intelligence; the curves
Of mouth and chin we thought so beautiful,
Are reproduced in her; but in her voice
There is a tone that thrills my every dream.
I know not why; but it doth seem so like—
So like a voice I 've heard before. Ah me!

Ernest. My brother—it doth seem so blest to call
Again thy name, and know that thou dost hear,

Now that returning health hath brought thee strength—
Tell me, I pray, these secrets of thy life
Whose poisoned fangs thus ever sting thy joys.

Thornton. How shall I tell thee, Ernest, all the shame
That I must bear to a dishonored grave?
How shall I wake within thy breast afresh
The answering shame that stung thine honest heart
When first thou heardst a rumor of my fall,
And knew the name thou bearest was disgraced.
My brother! O, my brother! better far
My form had lain beneath yon rolling waves
Than live to bring a blush upon thy cheek,
And wake contempt for me where love did dwell.

Ernest. Contempt, my brother? Nay. When first I heard
The tale, so many years ago, my heart
Did yearn with love and pity over thee;
And every eve and morning since, my prayer
Hath importuned the gracious ear of God
For thy return to home, and love, and peace.
O, fatal day! when thou didst leave the roof
Beneath whose shelter they abode with thee,
For one within whose sphere temptation lurked.

Thornton. Ay, fatal day, though beautiful it seemed.
My boyish heart was filled with wild delight,
To change the tameness of our country home
For the enchantments of the shifting scenes
Of crowded thoroughfares. A glorious life
Was pictured in my dreams—honor, success,
And most abundant wealth for manhood's years,
As the reward of very trifling toil.
I strove to do my duty, prospered well
Awhile, as thou dost know; but very soon
The Evil Eye, that hunts the souls of men,
Was fixed on me. My guardian was kind,
But filled with selfish cares; and I was left
To choose companions from the idle throng.
My books I never loved as well as thou,
And when the busy labors of the day
Were passed, and the long Winter evenings came,
The time grew heavy on my idle hands,
And I was but too glad when one did say,
"Come, go with us;" I asked not where, but went.
Alas! it is the tale so often told.
I followed others' paths, and never thought
Where they would lead. We gamed the nights away,

Nor blushed to find the solemn eye of Day
Upon our dissipation gazing sad.
I loved the game. It was the fatal rock
On which my gayly-sailing ship was wrecked.
The golden waves of each inflowing day
Did float some ragged fragment of my life,
To leave it, at the ebbing of its tide,
Stranded upon the shore—a sight for men
And God to gaze upon. I lost the trust
Reposed in me by those I served. At last
They could endure no more: I was expelled.
Thus left alone, destruction waited not.
Without employ, without a home or friend,
'T was then, in the despair that whipped my soul
To blindest fury, that I stole the name
I knew would bring me gold. Most precious gold!
I 'd make it serve me well, and ere 't was known
Cancel the evidence of crime, and strive
My sullied honor to reclaim. I said
It was discovery that made the crime,
And strove to cheat my conscience with the lie.
I sold the note that I had forged, and fled
Unto a distant city, changed my name,
And at the shifting wheel did strive again
My fortune to redeem. I staked my all;

My brains did seem on fire of hell. I played;
The cards were burning coals within my hand.
I felt afraid. It seemed as though my soul
Had linked its fate unto that pile of gold.
If I should lose! The room seemed full of smoke;
I could not breathe. If I should lose at last!
My limbs grew cold; I thought an evil form
Behind me stood, but dared not turn to see.
I knew the living God was in the room,
A presence terrible, whose calm, stern eye
Looked on, to see me game away my soul.
The game went on. Our mother came and stood
Where streamed the moonlight through a window-
pane,
And gazed, with look of sadness on the strife
For human souls. The game was o'er. I lost.
I dashed into the street. I ran, and ran,
I knew not, cared not whither—only cared
To rid me from the consciousness of guilt.
"Lost! lost!" I cried; "my soul is lost—is lost!"
At last the city far behind me lay.
I felt the cool air of the country blow
Upon my burning face. Beneath the stars—
The tender, pitying, Christ-revealing stars—
I felt the solemn beauty of the scene.

Moonlight and solitude! O, God is here,
I thought; not dreadful as in yonder den
Of thieves, but pitiful, most pitiful, and kind.
  I sank beside a blooming hedge, and said,
"Just over there is Paradise: I 'll wait
Here by the gate till God shall pass me by,
Then I will cry, 'Pity a soul that 's lost—
A soul for whom thy Son was crucified!'
And he can not deny." So wild my brain
With burning fever, and I knew it not.
I woke one day from long unconsciousness,
And found myself upon a curtained bed,
With watchers near. I had been found, they said,
Lying beside the hedge-row gate, and ill.
They nursed my gaining strength with such fond
    care
As they alone could give who do believe
And own the tender ties of brotherhood,
As universal as the race of man.
And then, as though God pitied me, and thought
To give my manhood one chance more to grow,
And bear the fruits of honesty and truth,
He opened wide these generous hearts to me,
So full of charity and gentleness,
And gave employment and prosperity.

I shunned companions, took myself to books,
And tried to gain the habits of a man.
But ah! my sin—how it did gnaw my peace,
Like some corroding cancer, night and day!
Did e'er a stranger cross my path, and look
Me sharply in the face, I thought, at last
Some officer of justice finds me out,
And, frightened, shied away, and tremblingly
Took up my duties. But the months rolled on,
And I grew calm and self-possessed at length,
And labored for the means with which to wipe
From record all the traces of my crime.
  But now the throbbings of another life
Began to warm my being. There was one,
A daughter of the house beneath whose roof
Such tender kindness had been shown to me;
And she was beautiful. Her face was rare
In its exceeding loveliness; her form
Preserved its grace in every supple move;
And there was in her voice a melody
That all my better nature did inspire.
I loved her as a man may love but one;
And she, just dawning into womanhood,
Returned my love with the pure strength of hers.
And she became my wife. O, God forgive!

E'en while the solemn vow was on my lips,
Remorse, with daggers keen, did probe my heart,
And the insulted angel of the shrine
Did snatch the chalice of my wedded joys,
And dashed it on the altar at my feet.
Unworthy of the blessed sacrament,
It was damnation to my guilty soul.
  Two years had passed—two years of agony.
The burning secret that I must conceal
E'en from my faithful wife, began to leave
Its traces on my frame. I did grow old;
Each passing month did leave the mark of years;
Until, one day, they placed within my arms
A little babe. My manhood left me then;
I wept the only tears my eyes had known
Since those that fell upon the violets
We planted on our mother's new-made grave.
My little child! And must her guileless soul
Be darkened by the shadow of my crime?
I prayed that she might die; but then I thought
God sent her as a token of his grace;
I will accept the gift, and, in his name,
I 'll go, confess my crime, for mercy ask,
And liquidate the debt, and from this hour
Be honest with mankind and with my God,

For her dear sake, and worthy strive to grow
Of those good blessings of the Father's hand.
I kissed my wife and child, with more of joy
Than I had known for years, bade them farewell.
"A few days' absence, and I would return,"
I said, and left them with elastic tread.
Ah! little did I know the heart of man!
I met my creditor. I trembled then.
He sat amid his bonds and mortgages,
Upright and stern in his integrity,
A man of honor, unimpeachable.
His face was thin and beardless; raven locks
Were neatly combed about a forehead low.
His nose was like a vulture's beak, his lips
Compressed and colorless, and 'neath his brows,
That rose and fell as his emotions changed,
There lay, like smoldering fires, his restless eyes.
Their gaze was fixed on me most dark and cold.
He heard my tale. "What was the need," he said,
"I should confess to him, who knew too well?"
"To make thee restitution I have come,"
I made reply, "and ask thee to forgive."
"Forgive!" he thundered; "I am not a God:
I never will forgive. There is a place
For such as thou, as thou shalt find full soon."

Wildly I prayed for mercy at his hand—
Mercy, for the dear sakes of wife and child;
For my own wretched soul; for love of Christ.
It was of no avail; he heard me not.
I was arrested, tried, condemned at last,
And forced within a prison's gloomy walls,
To spend the years that I had thought to fill
With virtuous deeds, to balance all my sin.
When first the ponderous door creaked on its hinge,
And, closing, shut between the world and me,
I sat upon my iron bed, and wept
Those bitter tears that bring us no relief.
They fell upon my heart like Winter sleet,
And clad it in an icy mail of hate.
I loved my wife and child, and for the sake
Of this sweet love I hated all the world,
Whose rules of justice thus had interposed
Between a life of virtuous bliss and me.
But past my tears, and in my wild despair
I stamped, and raved, and beat my prison bars
Until exhausted nature claimed her own;
And, sinking on my loathsome bed, I slept
A long, deep sleep, from which I woke, at length,
In calmer frame, and with a settled will

To scorn the hardness of my fate, and greet
With cold indifference every human glance
That met my own. But O, the hidden fires
That did consume me through those dreary years
In which I reaped the penalty of sin,
As though my heart had never felt the pangs,
My hand had never brought the fruits most meet
For deepest penitence!
It was not just,
I thought; and all the fountains of my life
Were turned to bitterness, save one alone:
My wife, my child—for them there bloomed, e'en
then,
One verdant spot, refreshed by waters sweet.
One thought there was that gave me keener pangs
Than all—the ruin I had brought to them
For whom I would have died a thousand deaths.
I knew her heart would break. My child would
learn
To hate her father's name; and I, at last,
Would step among mankind, a vagabond,
Despised of all.
Thus passed the years to me
Until the close of my imprisonment.
They changed my convict dress, and sent me forth

A stranger and before my time, white-haired
And old. I loitered not, but hasted on
To cast me at the feet of her I wronged,
And crave forgiveness and one gentle thought
From wife and child, if they could give no more.
I reached the mansion. Strangers trod the floor
Made sacred by her footsteps, and I heard
From them so sad a tale of changes strange
As would have wrung with pity alien hearts,
That fell on mine like burning coals upon
The living flesh.

Destruction came with one—
Thus ran the tale—whom from the street they took,
And nursed, and kept, with almost loving care.
He seemed most upright, and did woo and wed
The daughter, lovely as the Summer dawn.
But when their little child an infant lay
Within her nurse's arms, without a cause,
Save an impelling force of wickedness,
He did desert them all, nor came again.
The aged father died a bankrupt soon,
And they, the widowed and deserted, fled,
Whither, no one could tell. I staggered forth
Into the light that mocked me with its smile,
And, in my wretchedness, I prayed for death.

Ernest. Hadst thou forgotten, then, thy childhood's home,
And those who loved thee still so fondly there?
Thornton. Brother, I never did forget. 'T was shame
That kept me exiled all these years from thee,
That sent me wandering into distant lands,
And made me shrink from each repeated glance.
I 've traveled round the world, urged by the hope
That chance, or Providence—if such there be—
Might unto me reveal the hiding-place
Of my poor, wounded doe. But vain
Hath been my search; and when at last I found
My life was sloping to the grave, I came
To ask forgiveness of my kin, and die.
But shame and cold distrust still kept me back,
And I have lain within the shadows dear
Of these old walls all night, and at the dawn
Have crept away, fearing, yet wishing much,
To meet a face that I had seen before.
Often I 've met thy daughter as she passed,
Singing, along her happy ways, and sighed
To hear her sing, although I learned erelong
To listen for her voice as one doth list
The robin's note, after the Winter drear.

It seemed to me there was a prophecy
Of Spring in her glad song, so full of joy.
I knew she lived in the old homestead cot,
But little dreamed she was thy child. I feared
To ask for thee of those I daily met,
And had resolved to come, upon pretense,
And make inquiry of the gentle maid,
Whose low, sweet voice, I thought, might e'en console,
While it should speak new sorrow to my soul.

Ernest. And thou didst come, my brother, as the Lord,
According to the purpose of his love,
Did graciously direct. But I am sad
To hear this painful story of thy life
Since we did part; but far more sad am I
That darkened hath become the faith in God
That beamed upon thy boyhood's early morn
With radiance so beautiful and mild.

Thornton. I was alone, and all the world was cold.
Upon no household altar did there burn
For me a sacrifice at morn or eve.
While there was not a hand to guide my steps
Unto the sanctuary of the Lord,
A thousand clutching fingers drew me on

Unto the teeming haunts of wickedness,
And thus, an ever-yielding boy, I fell.
Then was I hated, mocked by God and man,
Scorned in my hour of deepest penitence,
Until at last, white-haired, I walked abroad,
A monument of wretchedest despair.

Ernest. My brother, O my brother! speak not thus.
The ever-pitying Christ will heed the prayer
Of weeping penitence. We are to him
As veins of his own body. All his heart
Is beating with the life of love for those
His own shed blood redeemed. Believe on him!
E'en now there waits for thee the Comforter,
Whose soothing voice, so full of tenderness,
Shall all the sorrows of thy heart console.
His breast invites thine aching head; his hand
Shall close thy wearied eyes with gentler touch
Than ever fondest mother knew, and thou
Shalt know again the bliss of peaceful rest.
O, love of Christ! Hath ever heart conceived
Its wondrous depths? its far outsweeping breadth,
As vast, as boundless as the wants of man?
He stoops to take the little, helpless child,
Left weeping by the way, unto his arms,

Giving the lonely one a parent's care.
The tottering feet of age he guides, upholds
The bowing form, and to the blinded eyes
Unfolds the glories of the world of light,
And all the sinful and the sorrowing
Are evermore remembered in his prayer
Of intercession at the Father's throne.
  Come thou! The weary wilds of earth too long
Thy feet have trod; too long thy parching lips
Have quaffed the waters of its brackish streams.
Here is a path, a fair and healthful way
Opened to thee. Here brightly-blooming flowers,
The lily-bells of peace, chime sweetly forth
Their invitation to most fragrant bowers,
Whence birds, in happy concert, call to thee.
The voice of heavenly pleasure bids thee come,
And duty, from a hundred unreaped fields,
Demands thy labor. And from far there comes,
Like the soft breathing of the Summer wind,
The murmured pleadings of thy mother's prayer,
That nightly, till her lips were cold and still,
Did hover round thy pillow, pure and sweet,
In holy benedictions, on the wings
Of faith, that wavered never from the word
Of promise, as the Rock of Ages sure.

She calls thee by those oft-repeated prayers,
And it were sad to bear upon one's soul,
Through all eternity, the fearful weight
Of an unanswered prayer.

Thornton. Stay, Ernest, stay!
I feel almost a little child again,
So filled with tender yearning is my soul.

Ernest. Of such is the Lord's kingdom, and except
Thou shalt become e'en as a child, thy feet
Unto its joys may never enter in.

SCENE XI.

VICTORIA IN A BOWER, WHERE STANDS A STATUETTE.

Victoria. My Cleone's gift to me! how beautiful!
His own dear hand did place it in this bower,
And twine these graceful branches of the vine
About the lovely brow. A poet's soul
Is thine, O my beloved—a poet's dream
Beneath thy hand hath found embodiment.
Genius hath crowned thee, and hath fondly clasped
The hand from which this fair creation sprung.
And thou wouldst give thyself, with all thy wealth
Of rare endowments, unto one like me!

Cleone. (*Entering.*) Ay, unto thee, beloved, and deem myself
In keeping all too sacred and too blest.
I can but think it is a cruel hand
That doth divide two hearts so closely bound
By love's most tender tie.

Victoria. A cruel hand?
Ah, Cleone! should the graceless stone complain
Beneath the chisel that, within thy hand,

Did from its roughness bring that lovely form?
These heavy chisel-strokes upon our hearts
Are needed much, to perfect in our lives
The image all divine that we must bear
Ere we shall stand within the garden fair
Of Zion's glorious King. O, let us wait,
With duteous love, upon our Father's will;
And, meantime, ere we claim another gift
From his most generous hand, with diligence
Perform the work that yet is ours to do.
Go thou, my Cleone: there 's a task for thee.
The world hath need of skillful hands like thine
To set these forms of beauty all along
Her ways, and educate the eyes of men,
Until the temple, place of toil, and home
Shall each the fair proportions take to please
The gaze refined, and correspond at last
Unto the model God before us placed
In his creation of this glorious world.
Go, with thy heart in sympathy with God's,
Thy hand by inspirations grand controlled,
And win the honors for thy name and art,
And praises for the Giver kind of all.
Chisel thy love, thy hope in spotless stone;
Teach patience to thy hand, faith to thy heart,

And thou shalt find in useful industry
The peace that is like balm to wounded souls.
Cleone. And thou?
Victoria. And I will wait, and hope, and pray.
Cleone. And love me still?
Victoria. Will love thee, Cleone, still.

Will love thee till those billows beat
Their rhythmic chant no more—
Till voiceless Silence waves her hand
From hill, and wood, and shore—
Till all the fountains of my soul
Are cold as polar snow,
I 'll love thee with the tenderest love
A woman's heart can know.

Cleone. Then will I go, commanded by thy lips,
And wait till thou shalt call the exile home.
I 'll wed me to my art, and faithfully
Will strive to gain the excellence I deemed
So little worth till now.
Yon airy form
To being sprung, my chisel from beneath,
When heart and hand thrilled with the touch of joy
That lent a grace to every careless stroke.
Now, for thy sake and God's, who lent this wealth
Of genius unto me, I e'en will wring

A truer grace from out the grip of toil,
And bring to thee, in this our trysting bower,
In that glad day, most full of bloom and song,
That God shall yet create for thee and me,
A token of my truthful, plighted faith.

Victoria. Go, Cleone; and God bless thee evermore.

Cleone. Ah! must it be? Farewell, beloved, farewell! (*Departs.*)

SCENE XII.

ERNEST AND VICTORIA.

Ernest. My daughter, did I hear thy step? I think
Thy foot doth fall more lightly on the floor
Than was its wont. Once did its happy tread
Sweep music from the grass it fell upon,
As it kept dancing measure to the songs
That dwelt upon thy lips, so glad and clear.
But now thy lay is sad and softly sung,
Like dirges at a grave. Come hither, child!
I have a thought that pains me: let me know
That it is groundless, and I am content.

Victoria. What is it, father? I am dutiful.

Ernest. Cleone hath not been here these many days,
And you are sad. You have not quarreled, love?

Victoria. Nay, father, nay.

Ernest. Ah! I am very glad.
Exacting often is the heart of youth,
And I did fear some sad, estranging cause

Had come at last between you twain for ill.
But wherefore comes he not? and why art thou
So all unlike thy former joyous self?
Victoria. Father, thou art my childhood's dearest friend,
The confident of my maturer years.
I loved my Cleone far too well to wed
My exiled life, so wrapped in mystery,
Unto the spotless honor of his name.
Most holy is the wedded state, and those
Who enter it should be not only one
In love, in faith, equals in intellect,
Possessed of kindred tastes, ambition, all,
But equal in their station 'mong the ranks
Of men. Believing thus, although my heart
Should break, I wait the providence of God.
I know his thoughts to us are all of love,
And that his hand may yet prepare the way
Unto the consummation of our hope;
And until then we are but lovers still.
Cleone hath genius and a work to do,
And he hath gone, at my request, awhile
To study sculpture in a school of art,
Until such time as I shall call him home.
This is the story, very simply told:

I love him as his worthiness compels,
With woman's truest heart; and I do think
I am more fit to live and do the will
Of God, since love so sweet did warm my heart
To higher life, though it should be in vain.
But I am sad—sometimes most sorrowful—
And were it not for that firm faith in God
That thou didst teach unto my infant heart,
I think I should repine in bitterness.
But it is well. The joys that o'er our paths
Do fall, like beams of sunlight, pleasingly,
Must have erelong their setting; dark and drear
Will be the night that follows, if we still
Do strain our eyes so for the brightness gone,
That all the glory of a thousand worlds,
Shining from far, unheeded falls around.
  But come, thou, take my hand, and we will tread
Again the dear familiar path that leads
Unto the peaceful city of the dead.
Still sacred and beloved to me the spot
That I have moistened with a daughter's tears;
And I would lay once more my wreath of flowers
Upon the hallowed mound, and weep and pray.
I still must call her mother, thou my sire,

And try to cheat my more than orphanhood
With the sweet music of an empty name.

Ernest. My daughter, oft I think this burden small
That the Lord's hand hath given thee to bear
Too heavily does rest upon thy head.
It was not meant to blight thy joyous years;
But as one oft transplants a lovely flower
From woodland, river-side, or garden fair,
That it may cause some desert place to bloom,
Thus was the changing of thy lot, I ween,
And it is sinful to repine or sigh
For a few blessings mayhap lost to us,
When all this glorious world of light and bloom
Is ours, and all the sky above our heads,
From which the Father's hand, so provident,
Daily doth drop unnumbered graces down.

Victoria. Forgive me, father, for those faithless words;
And thou, O Parent, far more tender still,
Forgive, I pray, thine oft-forgetting child!
I thank thee that my infancy was cast
Upon such loving hearts, so faithful hands,
That it did find a place so full of bloom,
Instead of some bleak desert place of sin,

Whose fierce sirocco, with its blast of death,
Had blighted every budding hope and love.
  But here 's the gateway, with its massive arch
By the triumphant ivy overtwined—
Most fit for those to pass beneath who gained,
In death, the one great victory of a life
Of conflict terrible and long. How sweet
The air, so laden with the breath of flowers,
And scent of new-made hay, from meadows near!
How softly sounds of distant labor fall,
Hushed to a sigh of rest, upon the ear,
Blending so soothingly with song of bird,
And dreamy chirp of cricket in the grass,
And murmuring of the waves upon the sand!
The brook that dances downward from the hill
So gleefully, with such a tread of mirth,
Here, as in sympathy with human hearts,
Glides softly out and in, the graves among,
With a low sound of tender melody,
As though it, sleeping, dreamed of heaven, and sang
The songs taught by the streams of Paradise.
  Ernest. Often thy hand hath led me o'er this path;
But soon, my daughter, thou shalt come alone;
Another grave shall claim thy reverent care,
And I shall sleep at last the quiet sleep

God giveth his beloved, by the dear side
Of her so early lost; and thou wilt come,
My child, some eve, and plant upon my grave
A few sweet flowers, those that I love so well,
And think of me, no longer blind and old,
But radiant with the bloom of perfect life
That all my veins shall thrill, with the first breath
Of air that fans me from the mount of God.

Victoria. Dear father, speak not thus: it wounds me so.

Ernest. Why should it wound thee? I am growing old:
The old must die, and now infirmities
Do press me onward to my resting-place.
Pray, what is death that we should fear it so?
'T is but a peaceful sleep when labor 's done.
'T is sad to those who yet are in their morn,
Their work but just begun; but in the eve,
When instruments of toil are laid aside,
And folded are the weary hands, 't is meet
That, with a prayer and hymn, we seek our couch,
And close our eyes in calm, refreshing sleep,
To wait the dawning of another morn,
When we shall wake, and, with new songs of praise,
Anew begin the holy work of God.

Victoria. Ah, father! that my heart were but more true
To heaven, and I could know, when life is dark,
That somewhere still the light doth shine for me!
But I forget, and sit me down and weep,
When I should take my little lamp of faith
In hand, and go about my Master's work.
But here are other mourners. There is one,
A slender creature, twining wreaths of flowers
Around a monument, spotless and fair,
Circled by many graves—one newly made,
On which she doth bestow most loving care,
While in a tender monotone she chants
A plaintive tune.

Ernest. Listen! we 'll pause to hear.

Woman. (*Reciting.*)

To the west of the field where we reap and sow,
'Mid the blooms of joy and the thorns of woe,
Stands a beautiful gate, with columns fair,
Uplifted high in the ambient air,
Whose bars of pearl and gold inclose
The wells of peace and the dale repose.

O, the air is rich with a rare perfume
That exhales from fields of fadeless bloom;
And the streams are fair in their living flow,
And the voice of their singing is sweet and low

As 't is sometimes borne to the listening ear
Of one who has wandered the portal near,
And with yearning heart doth watch and wait
For the angel that opens the Beautiful Gate.

It hath opened oft, and many feet
Have passed within to the still retreat,
Whose steps had lain close to our own,
And the gate was shut, and we toil alone
Till our task is done, and, hoping, wait
Till shall open for us the Beautiful Gate.

There was one we knew whose patient toil
Had wrung from the grasp of a stubborn soil
A harvest whose sheaves of ripened grain
Stood rich and fair o'er a golden plain.
He came at last, with his work all done,
As the west was tinged by the setting sun,
With a smile of peace, and a dear hand spread,
With a tender prayer, on a bowing head,
And passed to the joy, the peace, and rest
That is hidden deep in the valley's breast.
And we lingered still, to toil and wait,
Till should open for us the Beautiful Gate.

And but yestreen, as the sun had set,
While the faintest twilight lingered yet,
Again it oped, and we knew for one
Whose little day was scarce begun—
A tiny child, whose dreamy eyes
Yet held the light of Paradise.

———

We held him long, but he could not stay:
With folded hands he passed away,
Like a beam of light, or a pleasant dream
Wooed on by the voice of the garden stream.
He comes no more; and still we wait
Till shall open again the Beautiful Gate.

O, angel that stands at the Beautiful Gate!
How long must we labor, and watch, and wait?
Till the field is sown and the harvest done,
And the day is lit by a setting sun.
Then sweet, O reaper! the rest will be
That patience and toil shall win for thee!
O, the gentle touch of that balmy air
Shall smooth from thy brow each trace of care,
And the loved and lost to thy side shall spring
With the joys that eternal life doth bring.
Be patient; for rest and love await
Thy footsteps to enter the Beautiful Gate.

Ernest. That mourner needs no earthly comforting.
Blest are the eyes that through the mists of earth
Behold the arches of that gateway fair;
More blest when they shall gaze at last upon
The inner glory that the heart of man
Hath never yet conceived—eye never seen.

Victoria. There is thy brother, leaning on the stone

That rises o'er thy mother's sacred dust.
He seems to love this spot. Hither he comes
At early morn—at eve—to read and pray,
And cultivate the ground. His new-born love
And hope of heaven he here hath writ in flowers
Of softest tints. How he hath changed of late!

Ernest. Ay, he hath changed—so patient grown, so meek,
So filled with resignation to his lot!
I think the Spirit of the Lord hath set
His seal upon his brow. Thank God! thank God!

. . . .

Thornton. I wait, thee, Ernest, and thy faithful guide.
Take thou this seat within the willow's shade,
That I have built for thee to rest upon,
And we will spend the yet remaining hours
Of this calm afternoon in gentle talk,
Within the sanctuary of the dead,
A common love for whom hath drawn our feet,
From wanderings far and long, together here,
And that shall lay us side by side at last.

Ernest. My brother, all my heart hath joy to-day—
Joy in the presence of our household tombs,

That thou hast found at last the hand of Christ,
Whose strong, firm clasp shall draw thee up to God.

Thornton. And it is joy to me, whose heart hath felt
So keenly all the agony of sin.
I look astonished back to the abyss
From whence I came, so black with utter night,
So wild with winds, so cold with dashing rain,
And stand and breathe the sunshine and perfume
Upon this mount of God, and clap my hands,
And sing, because my heart is full of song.
But I am sad that all my many years,
Two score and ten, have borne no pleasant fruits.
I must begin my work. If I but sow
One little field for other hands to reap,
It still may yield a few rich sheaves at last,
That to the Lord may prove my gratitude
For his forgiving love and faithfulness.

Ernest. What wilt thou do, my brother? Tell me all.

Thornton. The will of God, whatever it may be,
Wherever it may lead, that would I do,
Proclaiming unto all I chance to meet
The message of his love. His love alone
Shall be my theme, so wondrous and so free.

This morning, sitting on the grave of her
Whose faithful prayer did haunt each midnight hour
Of all my sinful years, with these soft airs
Breathing an inspiration to my soul,
I thus did dedicate myself to God
In a melodious hymn, that she may sing
Who is the bird of thy sweet Paradise.

Victoria. (*Sings.*)

Father, whose love divine
Did o'er my pathway shine
  Through wandering years,
Whose hand did take my own
When all but life had flown,
Whose soft and gentle tone
  Did soothe my fears:

Savior, whose precious blood
For me so freely flowed
  On Calvary,
Whose brow with thorns was crowned,
Scourged, mocked, reviled, and bound,
Pierced through with many a wound,
  All, all for me:

Spirit of gentle might,
That, like a beam of light
  Holy and sweet,
Scattered the night away,

Brought in the perfect day,
Opened a better way
  Unto my feet:

Bring I this day to thee,
Humbly and gratefully,
  My offering—
All years I have to live,
All blessings thou shalt give,
Each grace I shall receive,
  These, these I bring.

Thornton. My song hath gathered sweetness
    from thy lips,
And comes with meaning new and beautiful
Unto my heart, translated by thy voice
Into the native language of the soul—
Music which thou hast learned so well to speak.
I love to hear thee sing. There is a power
In thy low voice I do not understand.
It e'en unmans me when I hear its tones,
My sole excuse for these unmanly tears.

Victoria. Nay, not unmanly are thy tears, I
    ween.
They do give token of a gentle heart,
Susceptible of Beauty's godlike power.
The Christ was gentle, and it doth become
Manhood in all its strength to be like him.

Would thou couldst hear my teacher sing! Her voice
Hath wondrous sweetness; but I think that soon
'T will swell the song they sing who are redeemed.
Thornton. Then is she ill?
Victoria. Ah yes! passing away,
And dying of a wounded heart, I think.
But she loves music as the angels do.
A few days since I sat beside her couch,
Beneath the open window. Near us stood
The old piano that she loves so well.
'T was open, that her eyes might catch the gleam
Of its white keys, whene'er she looked that way.
'T was like the smile of a congenial friend,
She said. She loved to lie and watch the ghosts
Of songs she used to sing, flitting among
The strings, that only need her skillful touch
To give them forms and voices as of old.
The sunlight through the half-closed shutter streamed
In one bright beam, wandered across the room,
And fell at last upon the finger-board,
And lingered there until at length I said,
"The sunlight comes to chide thine idle hands."
"Ah, chide me not," she whispered, "Lo, I send

The one most fit to be as in my stead."
She bade me go and play. I sat me down,
And lightly touched the sunlight-gilded keys,
When suddenly a quick, vibrating breath
Fell on my ear; I turned and looked at her;
She half reclined, and, with a pallid face,
Looked up and smiled a smile so sad and strange,
The while her breath came quick and eagerly.
I sat amazed that she, so ever calm,
So much was moved. "Fear not," at length she said;
"It is the soul of music that hath come
Upon that beam of light to occupy
The cords my hands shall wake to song no more.
It is the child I nursed so long ago;
Ah! it is bliss to hear her voice again."
She sighed, and on her pillow sunk, and lay,
With closèd eyes and slowly-moving lips,
Like one who murmured in a troubled dream.
Her mind had seemed to wander all the day,
And then I knew that she was crazed at last.
Ah me! that such a mind and such a soul,
Whose feet do stand so near the gates of heaven,
Should thus be darkened by the clouds of earth!
The saddest sight, save but a ruined soul,

Is that of intellect akin to God
In aspirations and in grasp of thought,
Bereft of reason, wandering up and down,
A star without an orbit, plunging on,
Through utter darkness, to an unknown fate.
  I go to her this eve, and thou canst lead
Thy brother home, thus speed me on my way.
Good-night, my father, and, dear friend, good-night.

SCENE XIII.

NIGHT. HERTHA ON A COUCH, HER MOTHER AND VICTORIA ATTENDING.

Hertha. (*Wanderingly.*) O, weary, weary feet! when shall ye rest?
Mother. Poor child! poor child!
Hertha. Ah, yes! poor little one!
How light the precious burden seems to me!
Poor child! with such a stain upon thy name,
Where can I hide thee from a scorning world?
What place of earth so sweet to thee and me
As were a quiet grave beneath the flowers?

(*Starting excitedly.*)

William! William! my Willie kind and true!
My husband, where art thou? O, come to me!
Mother. Hertha, my daughter, lay thy throbbing head
Here on thy mother's loving heart so true.
Hertha. A mother's heart! Do I not know its truth?

Mother. (*Soothingly.*) There! hush thee! hush!

(*Hertha sleeps.*)

Victoria. Ah! this is very sad!

Hertha. (*Suddenly waking.*) I 'm very ill! Send for a man of God.

Mother. (*To Victoria.*) For whom? The pastor is away, I hear.

Victoria. I know of one who is, I think, most fit
To minister to her, whose heart hath learned
The art of sympathy from sorrow's self,
Of consolation from the love of Christ.

Mother. Pray send for him.

Victoria. I will, right speedily. (*Leaves the room.*)

Hertha. (*Mournfully.*)

When, O, when will come the morning,
  And, with fingers tipped with bloom,
Fold back from the arch of heaven
  All this drapery of gloom?
O, my eyes are weary watching
  Through the darkening hours of night,
Peering eastward, watching, waiting
  For the coming of the light.

Morning! morning! vailed with glory,
  Wet with cooling dews and sweet,
Hasten o'er the hills of amber
  With thine ever-joyful feet!

Bind thy crown upon the mountains,
  And thy mantle on the plain,
Touch the breast of yonder robin
  That he wake, and sing again.

I have sat here in the darkness,
  Listening to the steps of Night,
As they steal about my chamber,
  Till my soul is filled with fright.

(*Enter Victoria and Thornton.*)

Hush! what means that stealthy rustle,
  And that creaking of the floor?
Hark! was not that sound a clicking
  Of the latchings of the door?

Hush, my fears! it is the throbbing
  Of my heart, and nothing more.
Would it were the hand of Lethe
  That I thought was at the door!
That she'd come, and, with her fingers
  Dipped in slumber's healing balm,
Bathe my eyes, and hush my spirit
  Into rest so sweet and calm.

But my soul is far too weary
  For a rest as sweet as this:
She would feel the glow of morning,
  Feel the sunshine's thrilling kiss;
Joy would rest and light would gladden;
  Peace, not Lethe, give me now;

Give to me the light of morning
  In my heart and on my brow.

Watching, waiting for the morning!
  Shall I wait and watch in vain?
Shall the darkness from my spirit
  Be uplifted ne'er again?
When shall ope the gates of heaven,
  O, my panting soul, to thee?
When shall bathe thine eyes from darkness
  In the morning's brimming sea?

Thornton. When Christ, who is our light, ariseth fair,
The glory of the morning comes apace,
Its light and bloom, its song and shout of joy.

Hertha. O, precious thought! O, holy name of Christ!
He is my light. But pray thou, pray for rest;
I 'm weary with this toil, and strife, and pain.

Thornton. (*Prays.*)

Father, thy Word hath promise made,
  "Come all ye unto me
  Who heavy-laden be,
  Who labor wearily,
 And I will give you rest."
 O, promise sweet and blest!
  Father, we come to thee.

Not as the little wandering child,
From fields where he had strayed,
Until the evening shade
Had made his heart afraid,
Comes to his mother's breast
For refuge and for rest—
Not thus we come to thee.

Not as the happy and the pure,
With meekly-closing eyes,
Come at the eventide,
From cheerful toil aside,
Where love and peace abide,
And joys of Paradise.
Not as they come for rest
Unto the tender breast
Of sleep, serene and blest—
Father, we come to thee.

But as the homesick wanderer comes,
Whose straying feet have prest
Full many a land unknown, to find
A country still more blest,
Till, with a whirling brain,
Weary with grief and pain,
Through chilling wind and rain,
Fainting, he turns again
To hearts that o'er him yearn,
Where through the windows burn
The lights of home, for rest.

Thus, as the weary come
To find a sheltering home,
  Father, we come to thee.

  We come to thee.
Although this earth of ours,
So beautiful with flowers,
With wreathing mists and showers,
With lips that smile, and eyes
That look through love's disguise,
Might seem a paradise;
  Yet here we find no rest—
No rest from care and pain,
No rest for heart and brain;
And now, in agony,
We come, O Christ, to thee!
And O, thou pitiful,
Thou ever merciful!
  We pray thee, give us rest.

Hertha. Dear Christ, I trust in thee. O, rest, sweet rest! (*Sleeps.*)

Victoria. (*To Thornton.*) Come thou, and look upon her face so fair
In its repose. (*Thornton bends over her.*)
How calm she sleepeth now!
Resting in her so childlike faith in Christ,
His name still dear when all else is forgot.

Thornton. (*Trembling with emotion.*) O God, 't is she!

Victoria. Thornton! what meaneth this?

Mother. (*Stepping forward.*)

Ah! then my faithful ear deceived me not;
And, William Thornton, thou art come at last,
Again to trample on our broken hearts!

Thornton. O, mother! can it be?

Mother. Mother to thee?

Thornton. O, scorn me not! But come thou here with me,
And list to the sad tale I have to tell. (*They withdraw.*)

Victoria. O, mystery! Father, thyself reveal
In these unfoldings of thy Providence.
Poor, wounded heart! and sadly-wandering brain!
May some sweet balm of healing for thee flow
From those pierced branches of thy tenderest love,
And of those blooms thou long hast mourned as lost
Some crown of peace for thine own brow be twined!

SCENE XIV.

THE MOTHER AND THORNTON.

Thornton. Thou 'st heard the tale, so full of shame and crime;
But canst thou not forgive? O, I have paid
The penalty of sin in agony
Unmeasured by the flight of years. My heart
In its pure love for her hath changeless been,
And faithful as the planet to its sun.
I 've searched her round the world, and now at last,
As I have found her on the river's brink,
Whose waves must roll between our hearts so soon,
For the dear love of Christ, do not deny
This little boon, to hold her in my arms
Until the rising flood shall bear her hence—
Once more to call her by the holy name
Whose tender melody hath thrilled my dreams,
And woke my heart anew, each rising morn,
To bitterest regret and saddest tears.

Mother. (*Weeping.*) I must forgive the penitent who claims

The name of Christ. But O, my child! my
child!
My son, forgive the mother's anxious heart;
But once I gave in confidence to thee
The only treasure of my wedded life:
And thou dost know how soon, without a word
Explaining aught, she was returned to me
Disfigured, in the arms of agony.
I prest her to my breast and wept, and said,
"My bird, here fold thy wounded wing,
From the calm ether that did tempt thee forth
By rushing winds and sharply-driving hail
Beat back unto the parent nest again."
Blame thou me not if, fearing, tremblingly
I yield, and give her once again to thee.
But we will to her room—she may awake.

Thornton. Yet stay thou: I have still one thing
to ask.
Where is my child? O, tell me she yet lives!

Mother. She lives; but where, I may not tell
thee now.

Thornton. Wherefore? I have a right to know
it all.

Mother. The mother's lips must tell thee of the
child.

Thornton. I wait; but ah! my wild, impatient
heart!
We will return again. Lead thou the way.
Mother. Be very calm. Control thy eager lips.
The balmy sleep that o'er her fell is hope.
By all thy love for her, I charge again,
Await the dawning of intelligence,
And then deal gently with the broken heart.
Not much of joy or sorrow could she bear.

(*They enter. Thornton, kneeling by the bedside, prays silently.*)

Mother. She sleepeth still?
Victoria. As calmly as a child.
A gentle moisture rests upon her brow,
And the physician, who did call just now,
Said there was much to hope from such a sleep.
I pray the Lord her reason come again
For sake of the sad weeper at her side.
Thornton. (*Still kneeling.*)
O, gracious Father, save her—save, I pray!
Give back my wife to me—my wife and child—
And let me know at length, before I die,
The sweet enjoyments of a holy love.
One look of recognition grant from her,
And words of kind forgiveness and of hope.

Nevertheless thy will, not mine, be done.
I yield my will, for it hath wrought but woe,
And well I know thine is alone but love.

Hertha. (*Waking.*) Mother!

Mother. What is it, love? I'm at thy side.

Hertha. Yes, thou art ever near, most kind, most true.
I think the time must come erelong to close
This strife with life and death.

Thornton. God, hear my prayer!

Hertha. Whence came that voice? I thought it had a tone
That I had never thought to hear again.

Mother. A friend, my child, led here by Providence.

Hertha. A friend? Ah, mother! all thy face betrays
A secret thou wouldst keep. 'T is he! 't is he!

Thornton. Hertha, my wife! it was thy husband's voice.

Hertha. My husband's voice? At last! at last! thank God!

Thornton. Ah yes, thank God! For evermore be praised,

O Thou, whose name is graciousness and love!
But tell me, dearest, hath thy love outlived
The ruthless trampling of a score of years?

Hertha. My love is deathless as the soul; but ah!
The weary, weary waiting! Tell me all.

Thornton. Not yet, beloved. Thou hast not strength to hear
So sad a tale. Rest here within my arms,
That e'en have won the right to hold thee thus
Through sorrow deep as human heart could bear.
But that is past—how, thou shalt know erelong.
But ah! my wife, I fain would clasp our child.
Thy mother tells me she yet lives—but where?

Hertha. (*Reaching her hands toward Victoria.*)
Come hither, child: the hour at last hath come.

(*Victoria, bewildered, hesitates.*)

Mother. Victoria, thy mother calleth thee.

Victoria. My mother calls me? can it be? ah no!

Hertha. My husband, here behold thy child. My child,
At length thy mother know.

Victoria. What meaneth this?
My mother and my father? Ah! my brain
Is whirling now—I understand you not.

Thornton. Delude me not: she is my brother's child.

Hertha. Thy brother's child? Who is thy brother, pray?

Thornton. Blind Ernest Raymond, whom this maiden calls
Her father; mine own mother's son is he.

Hertha. But she is not his child. List thou to me.

Mother. My daughter, rest thee. Thou art far too ill.
I will explain, in a few simple words,
All that is known.

(*To Thornton.*) When thou didst come no more,
Racked with suspense, anxiety, and dread,
Her reason flickered, like a fannèd flame.
At first we thought thee dead. Then rumors came
That settled in our minds the sad belief
Of thy desertion and of our disgrace;
And in a strange, wild way she moaned and sighed,
Lamenting that her child should live to share
The dark dishonor of her mother's name.
My husband died, and we were left alone,
And, in my own bereavement and distress,
I did neglect awhile my ceaseless care
Of her, and woke one morn to find her gone—

Her and the child—and whither none could tell.
With almost wingèd speed the land was searched,
The woods, the mountains, valley, river—all
Were hunted o'er and o'er. It was in vain.
We found her not.
One eve I sat alone
In the old room that had been hers, and wept.
I felt most desolate, and thought that God
His presence had withdrawn from me for aye,
When a light footstep fell upon my ear.
I turned, and Hertha stood—her shadowed self—
Before the mirror, drawing off her gloves.
Her face was deadly pale; a lurid flame
Burned in her eyes; her long, unkempen hair
Hung, like a mass of black and rumpled crape,
From underneath her hat; and she had come
Alone! No infant form was on her breast!
Where was the child? I questioned her in vain:
She stared upon me with her glaring eyes,
And knew me not.
It were too long to tell
Of the five years that passed from that sad time;
The weary searching for the missing child,
That I could not believe as dead; the strife
For reason in her mind, so pitiful

To see; the dawning hope, so hailed with joy;
At last the restoration sure, but slow,
When she was given back to me again,
My child, my loving child, e'en as before.
One thing was strange, and marked the place where God
Had folded down a leaf. All else forgot,
She held in her remembrance faithfully
Her sorrow and the parting with her child.
She said that from some impulse, strange and quick,
She lay her, sleeping, in a flowery spot,
Where she had seen a woman, with a face
Most motherly and kind, at work one day,
And, hiding, waited till she bore her in,
Then frighted fled, whither she did not mind.
This was the time when all of earth was gone,
And she had learned how weak she was alone,
That she did take the proffered arm of Christ
To lean upon, and found it sure and strong.
At length, when came sufficient strength to her,
We started forth to find the child again.
We reached the village inn one afternoon,
And waited in the parlor for a space,
When there did pass along upon the street
A blind man, guided by a little girl

Some six years old. A lady sitting near
Did make remark, "Blind Raymond and his guide."
"His child?" I asked. "Ah! thereby hangs a tale,"
She made reply; "it is a child they found,
Five years ago, upon the garden path.
But he does call her his. He says the Lord
Did send her, and it seemeth so to me;
For he—poor man!—was comfortless before.
His wife was dead, and he, childless and blind,
Without a thing to love, with but the hand
Of servitude to guide him on his way.
But since she came he hath grown reconciled;
And now I think no face more full of smiles,
No heart more full of grateful joy than his
Doth greet the light, as, with the tiny palm
Of that fair child most fondly clasped in his,
He daily takes his recreative walk.
He hath abundant wealth, and she hath found
The tenderest guardians for her helplessness.
But I do think he would most surely die
Should aught remove his little blessing now."
The story ended, she passed on her way.
"Hertha, what shall we do?" I asked at length.
"Nothing to-night," she said, and craved a room.

All night she bowed upon the floor in prayer,
While I reclined, but not to sleep. At morn
She rose, and bathed her hueless face, and said,
"Mother, that poor old man hath won a right
To her, cast on his generous charity
When she did need a mother's tenderest care,
(I can but think it was the Lord indeed
That hid her from the blast that drove me wild,)
And it were cruelty to rob him now,
When he hath need of her. This will I do,
Conceal my true relationship to her,
Establish me a school, and strive to gain
The child's attendance, thus her teacher be,
Until I may, with better right, resume
The mother's sacred name." And it was so.
Through all these years with faithfulness she taught
The unsuspecting girl, treasured as pearls
The words that did reveal her glowing love
For her dear teacher, each caress received
As though it might a stolen pleasure be,
The while she pined to hear her speak the name
Most fit for her to bear. My heart hath said,
Full oft, This is not right—it is not right!
But she did think it was the will of God,
And heeded not her spirit's yearning cry.

Hertha. It was His will. O, see what it hath wrought!

Victoria. And this is true?

Hertha. All true—all true, dear child.

Victoria. (*Embracing her.*) My mother! mother!

Hertha. Call me thus again.

Victoria. Mother! 'T is sweet to speak that name to thee.

Thornton. My wife—my daughter, thus to me restored!
O, Lord, my thanks are broken by my joy,
Like prism-shattered beams of light; but thou
Canst read the language of each several ray;
And thou dost know my fervent gratitude.
I take, only to yield again to thee.
Keep thou my treasures, for my grasp is frail:
In keeping, draw us all more near to thee.

Hertha. Amen!

Victoria. How God hath ordered all our ways!
Here husband, wife, parents and child are found,
Three raveled lives together knit again.
My heart gives praise to him.

Thornton. All praise to him!
To us the joy.

Hertha. The peace, the rest, the joy!

SCENE XV.

CLEONE IN VICTORIA'S BOWER. BESIDE HIM A LIFE-SIZED STATUE OF HER STANDING ON A BEACH, WITH A SEA-SHELL IN HER HAND.

Cleone. And thus I come at last. O, it is bliss
To know I am so near to her, my soul's beloved!
Since last I stood within this bower with her
One year ago, how all my life hath changed!
Then from between these intertwining vines
I looked forth on a lonely world with dread.
I went at her behest, and found a life
Infusing all, of which I had not dreamed—
A life of joy, that flowed from Labor's heart.
I linked the vein that disappointment rent
To his; the quickening tide inflowed, and filled
Me with a manhood I had never known.
And so I am returned; and once again
I stand in this familiar place, and look,
With eyes that God hath touched, upon the world
Where shine the footprints of his providence;
And now I know it was God's voice that spoke

From out her lips, and bade me go and toil,
That I might win the gladness of this hour.
But ah! I catch the gleam of a white robe
Upon the porch, and there, amid the vines,
I see a hand that flutters like a dove.
A shower of snowy petals falls around;
A cloud of perfume floats upon the air.
She plucks a flower: it will be mine erelong;
And now she passes down the path, and comes,
Most perfect in her ripened womanhood,
To me, the queenliest, noblest one of all.
Victoria! (*Advancing toward her.*)

Victoria. My Cleone, thou art come?

Cleone. I e'en must come when thou dost call, beloved.
Full long I 've waited for thy messenger,
And when it came, my footsteps tarried not,
And now I think the hand I hold is mine.

Victoria. Thine, dearest, by the grace of God alone.

Cleone. A gift of God! Most fit to be bestowed
By Him who gave the flowers, the birds, the stars,
And all things beautiful and good; and now
Beneath the solemn glory of thy heavens,
I promise thee, kind Giver, to be true

Unto the trust thou hast reposed in me.
With gladness I will recompense her life
For every pang of sorrow she hath known,
And with her wealth of strength and hope enriched,
Of my own life will build unto thy name
A temple fair and beautiful to see.
Truly "thy loving-kindness crowns our days."

Victoria. But there are others who do wait for thee.

Cleone. Ah yes! and I would greet them. We will go.
How strange this story of thy life, beloved!
To think she is thy mother, he thy sire!
But now I know ye two are not unlike;
And I have wondered often at the sound
Of her voice, and of thine, so like are they
As oft to cheat the most familiar ear.
But she was ill, and very near her grave.

Victoria. Grief was her malady, and joy did prove
The best physician in her case, and now
The rose doth bloom most freshly on the cheek
Where then the lily of the shadowed vale
Its hueless petals spread. O, it is sweet
To call her mother! Dearest, holiest name!

And all the world hath gathered manliness
From the most noble presence of my sire.

Thornton. (*Approaching with Hertha and Ernest.*)
And gladness from my daughter's happy voice.
But this is he whom we must welcome home.

Cleone. Sweet is a welcome at these hands of yours.

Thornton. Gladly we greet thee for her sake, dear friend.
Because of us ye two have suffered much,
And it doth add a sweetness to our joy
That we at last may give thy bride to thee.

Hertha. Nay, Thornton, nay. Whose truest love hath kept
Her through these years? His is the right to give.

Thornton. Dear Hertha, true. My brother, she is thine.

Ernest. I will accept the gift of generous love.
Long since I gave her unto him, but then
I did not know one-half his worthiness.
That he hath nobly proved, and now, again,
With richest blessings of an old man's heart,
With prayers for all the sweetest gifts of Heaven
To crown your lives, I give thy bride to thee.

Victoria. But I do crave my mother's blessing now.

Cleone. And I. God make me e'en a son to thee!

Hertha. (*Clasping them in her arms.*)

Grace be unto you, my children,
  From the Father of us all!
Softly as the dew of evening,
  May it on your spirits fall!
May the peace that dwells with Jesus,
  That alone can make you blest,
From the heaven above descending,
  Fold its wings upon your breast,
And your spirits, like the waters
  Of the sacred Galilee,
When the Master stilled the tempest,
  Ever calm and peaceful be!

Thornton. O, holy blessing of a mother's heart!
It comes with fragrance from the mount of God.

Victoria. (*To Cleone.*) But thou didst give a pledge
    when we did part
That at thy hand awaits fulfillment now.

Cleone. Come ye with me. (*They enter the bower.*)
    She sent me forth to toil.
I do suspect my idleness did shame
Her so industrious hands. She bade me carve
My hope, my faithful love, in spotless stone,
And lo! I bring the product of my hands.
Her form—the dear embodiment of all

I hope and love beneath the heavens and God;
For its expression, as most fit, I chose,
As once I saw her stand upon the beach,
Gazing upon the glory of the heavens,
While in her palm a rosy shell did lie.

Victoria. Dear Cleone, thou didst see with lover's eyes,
And with a lover's partial hand hath wrought;
For this is beautiful.

Cleone. Here standeth one
Who can not be deceived. Friend Raymond, tell
If with a partial hand I carved this face,
This form. Thy touch so sure would soon detect
A single deviation from the truth.

Ernest. (*Passing his hand over the face.*)
That thine is an impartial hand, I fear,
It were not well for one who loves the truth
To say; but I am witness to its skill.
The low, broad forehead, with its penciled brows;
The smoothly-rounded temples, large, full eyes;
The swelling of the cheek; the nose, the mouth,
The chin; these all are hers—peculiar each to her.
The ear, half hidden 'neath the rippling hair,
Whose graceful folds adorn a noble head,
I know them well; and ah! that hand I know;

But it is cold—so cold! Victoria,
Give me thy warm and living hand again.
Thy chisel hath most faithful been, my boy;
But thou couldst not bestow the warmth of life,
And it is cold—so cold! Pray lead me in.

SCENE XVI.

MORNING. ERNEST ON A COUCH. THORNTON, HERTHA, CLEONE, VICTORIA AND RUTH ATTENDING.

Ernest. Open the shutter, that the blessed sun
May lay his warming hand upon my brow.
Victoria. Dear father, art thou cold?
Ernest. Yes, very cold.
But that must be: all earthly fires must die;
All passion heats must chill within this frame
Before the purer life we live in God
Can flow into my veins. I am content to die.
In darkness I have trod the ways of earth,
Ofttimes in utter weakness and in fear;
And it is joy to me to know that soon
The quick, effulgent glory of the day
Of which Jehovah is the sun shall dawn
Upon my darkness, and dispel its gloom.
O, fragrant breath of flowers! It cheers me still
To know that flowers do bloom. Pluck me a sprig

Of morning-glories from the vine Ruth trained
About the porch. O, I am glad to know
I leave the earth so beautiful at last,
That when my soul shall, disembodied, spring
Toward the throne of God, its pathway lies
Through sunshine and perfume.

Thornton. A fairer world
Awaits thee. Soon thine eyes shall look upon
Those fields of fadeless bloom and rivers clear;
And, more than all beside, thou shalt behold
The face of Jesus in its loveliness.
Does this thought give thee joy?

Ernest. Ay, fullest joy.
O Jesus, Jesus! best beloved of all!
'T is sweet in thine embracing arms to lie,
And know that in my own poor life thy will
To its accomplishment goes on.

Dear friends,
How the good will of Christ hath wrought itself
Into the somber texture of our lives—
A thread of gold, in patterns beautiful
As his own lilies of the field. See how
Amid the darkness of her widowed years
It shines—the Star of Bethlehem, whose beams
Hath overreached her life, and fallen upon

The pathway of us each, a ray of hope.
It gives me joy thus to depart at last
From this dear home, and know that peace remains
Beside the hearth, to give you comfort still.

(*Ruth, bending over him, drops a tear on his face.*)

Whence came that tear? Whose eyes will dare to
weep
When he who hath been blind receives his sight?

Ruth. Dear master, pray forgive old Ruth the
tear.

Ernest. My faithful Ruth, I do commend thee now
Unto the care of better hands than mine.
My child—Victoria—remember her!
But there 's no need to charge thy loving heart:
Thou never couldst forget.

Victoria. Nay, father, nay.

Ernest. And thou, dear child, thy hand is clasped
in mine
For the last time, and not to lead me now.
A stronger arm than thine I lean upon
As I descend into the shadowed vale.
This is the clasp of loving friends, who part
With hope to meet again. God bless you both,
My children! In your lives accomplish all
His will—his will, so full of perfect love.

My brother—sister—let me take your hands.
Just one clasp more.
Jesus—Jesus, my Light!
The glory of thy coming dawns apace.
He comes: his hand hath touched my eyes! I see!
I see you all—and Jesus in the midst!
Farewell, loved ones of earth; I go to him.

Hertha. (*Bending over him.*) Ah! he hath gone!

Thornton. Yes, he will grope no more
Darkly the ways of earth—he lives in heaven.

Victoria. His hand did write his own sweet epitaph
In those fair flowers he still so closely clasps.
(*Closing his eyes.*)
Dear, darkened eyes! your night is overpast,
And morning-glories bloom at last for you.
Brave heart, silent and cold—thou to thy rest,
We unto labor only just begun.

Cleone. Lo! for the righteous light is sown, and joy
For those who walk in their integrity.
Golden the harvest stands o'er yonder plains
Whither he goes to reap.
Gladness and light!
O, heir to such inheritance, we bid thee joy!

Victoria. Ay, joy; for looking onward through our tears
Along the path that thou hast humbly trod,
We trace thy footsteps parallel with Christ's.
The grave o'er which he triumphed waits for thee,
The home that he went onward to prepare,
And the eternal life of joy, of which
The heart of man hath never yet conceived.
O, may I ever follow thee, as thou
Didst meekly follow Christ, and win at last
The right to bear my name—VICTORIA!

MISCELLANEOUS POEMS.

MISCELLANEOUS POEMS.

MISCELLANEOUS POEMS.

THE THRESHOLD.

It may be a block of marble
  At the rich man's palace door:
At the peasant's humble cottage
  Just a stone, and nothing more;
But each threshold hath a story
  Of the feet that trod it o'er;
Many have a sad remembrance
  Of the feet that come no more.

There is one my memory seeth,
  Shaded by a maple-tree,
Over which our feet went dancing
  With a tinkling sound of glee—
In and out with ringing laughter,
  Out and in the livelong day,

Till two crossed a grassy threshold
  Starred with daisies by the way,
Leaving us outside, awaiting
  For the opening of the door
That we knew would open to those
  Footsteps never, nevermore.

O, how pallid looked the sunshine
  As it crept the threshold o'er!
And how dreary seemed the shadow
  Of the maple by the door!
And how long the hours lingered,
  As if saddened by our woe,
While our feet, timed to the beating
  Of our hearts, went sad and slow—

Till at last we crossed the threshold,
  Passed the maple by the door,
Left the haunted crescent cottage,
  To return again no more—
Left it, haunted by the memories
  That still cross the threshold stone—
Out and in, forever talking
  Of the inmates that have gone!

Now our feet cross other thresholds—
  Some the one that 's made of gold,
Through the door that leadeth into
  Joys that tongue hath never told;
And with hearts forever yearning
  For the loved who 've gained their home,
Others wearily are treading
  'Mid earth's busy ways alone.

But we think, while we are passing,
  Sad and tired, on our way,
With our broken home behind us,
  Where the lights of memory play,
Of the one that 's just before us,
  That the morning shineth o'er,
From whose fair and golden threshold
  We shall wander nevermore.

SABBATH MORNING AT LEAF RIVER

It is morning. I sit where the stream
  With the sunlight drawn close to its breast,
Flows sparkling away to the mill,
  With its murmur of cheerful unrest.

There 's a song on the lips of the wave
  That is wonderfully soothing and sweet,
And a melody follows the tread
  O'er the stones of its white foamy feet.

And it speaks to my spirit this morn,
  While the Sabbath bends over the stream,
With an influence holy and sweet
  As the song that may float through a dream.

O, the music that chimes in the waves,
  And the echo that sings in my soul,
And the Sabbath that holdeth the earth
  And my spirit in peaceful control!

And the sunlight that seems like a smile
  From the reconciled face of our God,
As it falls on the earth, through whose ways
  The footsteps of beauty have trod!

The forest is stretching away
  With its banners of crimson and gold,
And the mirroring waters beneath
  Other Autumn-dyed forests unfold.

There 's a glory above in the sky,
  And a glory dwells under the stream;
'T is the garment that nature hath wove
  For the child of her artistic dream.

But the song that is sung by the stream
  As it dances away to the mill,
Shall be hushed on the lips of the wave,
  All the waters be lifeless and still,

And the glory that filleth the earth
  Be shrouded in darkness for aye,
When the breath of Jehovah shall sweep
  The strength of the heavens away.

But the light that is shining within,
  And the song that is sung by the soul,
Shall grow brighter and sweeter for aye,
  While the years of eternity roll.

LITTLE JULIA.

CAME she to my lonely chamber,
  Softly, every Summer day
Bringing, hid beneath her apron,
  Prairie-flowers so bright and gay.

There they stood upon the table
  As she grouped them in the vase,
Roses wild, receiving beauty
  From her touch so full of grace.

Dear to me the gentle flowers,
  With their forms so bright and fair;
But unto my heart lay nearer
  The loved hand that placed them there.

I can ne'er forget how sweetly
  Beamed her eyes of heavenly blue,
Or how quickly timid blushes
  Overspread the lily hue.

Of her cheek, as shyly waiting
  On the threshold of the door
For the ever-ready welcome
  That she will receive no more.

Thus she brought her fragrant offering
  On that lovely Summer day,
Roses wild, that her small fingers
  Twined into a sweet bouquet.

Gentle Julia! She was fairer
  Than those blooming flowers to me;
And she was more frail—they faded
  Not away so soon as she.

Bitter fell my tears, and swiftly,
  When she died one Summer day,
And I treasured long the flowers
  That had formed her last bouquet.

Long a sweet, delicious perfume
  Hovered o'er their withered bloom,
Just as hope that 's born of heaven
  Lingers round an infant's tomb.

And I knew that little Julia
  Gathered flowers she loved so well
On the glorious plains of heaven,
  Where all things of beauty dwell.

THE OLD "NORTH ROOM."

It is eventide. I am sitting here
In the old "north room," that has grown so dear
Through the years that my feet have pressed the floor,
Passed in and out at the open door—
Through the years that have passed 'neath the humble roof,
And flung o'er the walls such a checkered woof—
A woof inwove with blight and bloom,
With December snows and the leaves of June.

'T is the same old room. O'er the mantle-tree
Hangs the pictured face that has looked at me
So many years, with that earnest gaze
That seemed to be guarding all my ways;
And the books I read in the Summer hours
Are strewn around among fragrant flowers;
And in the corner the old arm-chair
Yet stands; but *he* is no longer there.

'T is the same old room; but awhile ago
There were many feet to come and go,
And these walls were filled, from morn to night,
With happy voice and footfall light.
But the tide of laughter has ebbed, and we
Find moaning shells where it used to be,
And the footfall light has passed away,
And the house is still and lone to-day.

The face there pictured youthful, now
Bears the stamp of years on the lofty brow.
In a distant home, with a fonder gaze,
Those eyes now guard another's ways,
The while from the place o'er the mantle-tree
They seem to be watching no one but me,
And the form that reclined in the old arm-chair—
Do you see yon grave? It resteth there.

'T is a haunted house, and, lingering near,
Are forms whose voices I always hear;
And the shadows that flit around my chair
Bear the beautiful faces they used to wear;
And so our house, though still and lone,
Hath many dwellers and many a tone;

But they speak alone to the listening ear—
To the watching eyes alone appear.

So I sit and listen, and watch and wait,
And I think of the beautiful pearly gate—
Of the region beyond, the sparkling river
Where the sun for aye unbinds his quiver,
Where the air is life, and the life is song,
And the song is a joy their lips prolong;
And I seem e'en now to hear the strain
Of the loved who lived, nor lived in vain.

And this eventide, while sitting here
In the old north room, it hath grown more dear;
For the feet of the shadows that pressed the floor,
Passed in and out at the open door—
For the shadows that passed 'neath the humble roof,
And flung o'er the walls such a beautiful woof—
A woof inwove with a fadeless bloom,
With leaves more fair than the leaves of June.

BIRDIE AT PRAYER.

"Now I lay me"—it is Birdie,
  With her voice so low and sweet,
Murmuring that prayer of childhood,
  Kneeling at our mother's feet.
Gently clasped her dimpled fingers,
  Round her falls a robe of white,
While her blue-veined lids droop lightly
  O'er her eyes so softly bright.

Heaves her breast with purest pulses,
  And her lips are just apart,
While that prayer floats out, as fragrance
  Cometh from a rose's heart;
And the softest airs of heaven
  Wait to bear it to the throne,
As the sighing winds of Summer
  Bear the sweets by roses blown.

Gushing with the young heart's beating
  Upward through the blushing lips,
Thrilling other hearts, and vailing
  Eyes with tears in sweet eclipse,
Floating upward through the ether,
  Pulsing through the heavenly air
Till it finds the heart of Jesus,
  Goes that infant's evening prayer.

O, how sweet the cord that bindeth
  Hers to that great heart of love,
Whose pulsations send the life-blood
  To each soul beneath, above!
And whose love is ever o'er us
  As we wander through the wild,
Watching with unuttered yearning
  O'er each straying, erring child!

And as every evening foldeth
  Up that heart to sweet repose,
And that prayer ascends, as fragrance
  Cometh from the folding rose,
How that cord of love shall strengthen—
  Every prayer a golden strand,

Drawing that sweet spirit upward
  To the better, holier land!

Blessed Savior! all her footsteps
  Till life's dusky evening keep,
Then, white-robed and sweetly praying,
  May she "lay her down to sleep,"
Knowing that, when passed the night-time,
  When the glorious morn shall break,
In thy likeness, in thy glory,
  In thy joy, she shall awake!

THE DYING MISSIONARY.

It was evening—the hands of the shadow
Gathered up the bright robes of the day,
With the reverent care of a mourner,
And tearfully laid them away.

And silence came down o'er the city,
And hushed was its sad, restless moan,
And the gods that it worshiped were standing
By rites all deserted alone.

But the One whom those rites had insulted
Still watched, with his pitying eyes,
O'er the hearts from whose night-templed altars
No incense to him did arise.

Yet a voice from the stars sang his praises,
And a chorus by ocean was sung,
And the flowers, by the hands of the breezes,
Like censers, were noiselessly swung.

And thus came the peace of the evening,
  And its sweet, dewy blessings did fall
Alike on the heathen and Christian;
  For the good Father careth for all.

'T was then in the evening of nature,
  A soul to its morning drew nigh;
The stars of the earth-life were paling
  At the glory that dawned in the sky.

The messenger's feet had grown weary
  While the "good news" was yet on the tongue,
And the song was completed in heaven,
  That on earth was so sweetly begun.

They were standing around her in silence,
  But each heart heard its own bitter moan,
That brave mission band, calmly waiting
  The stroke that should leave them alone.

Not *alone*—for the voice that had bid them
  Go forth on that dark weary way,
Now whispered, "In faith be believing,
  For lo! I am with you for aye."

And they reached out the hand of the spirit,
For the night of their sorrow was deep,
And cried, "O, our Father! our Father!
The way of our footsteps still keep."

How the dear eyes were dimming and failing!
And the sweet lips were fearfully white
As they murmured, "The hymn that is dearest,
O sing, as I pass through the night."

And that clear song of triumph rose upward,
And blent with the song of the spheres,
And the sweet balm of healing descended,
And soothed all their sorrowing tears.

"I leave the world without a tear,
Save for the friends who linger here!"
'T was thus they sang, and on her sight
There burst the glorious morning light,
And with the last sweet note she fled—
They stood alone beside the dead.

Like a calm wave that seeks the sea,
Her spirit passed away,

And left upon each cheek a tear
For those who lingered weeping here,
    Like drops of dewy spray.
And sanctified and glorified,
'T was thus she calmly, sweetly died,
Leaving the world without a tear,
Save for the friends that linger here."

MY SHELLS.

I STOOD beside Love's brimming sea;
The bright waves broke in melody
On golden sands, close up to me.

More beautiful the waters seemed
Than maiden heart had ever dreamed,
As over them the sunlight beamed.

The waves brought treasures from a land
Afar, to many an outstretched hand
Of those who waited on the strand.

To one, sprigs of anemone;
A gem, to one, most fair to see;
Two little shells, at last, to me.

Two little shells, as snow-flakes white,
Whose lips, kissed by the rosy light,
Were flushed with crimson, soft and bright.

And from their lips there came a tone
So low and sweet—half song, half moan—
Learned of the ocean's waves alone.

And all day long, beside the sea,
Entranced by the strange melody,
I sat, and heard them sing to me—

Until they to my heart had grown,
Until I claimed them for my own,
And they and I were only one.

They were not mine, alas for me!
The waves rolled high, and angrily
Bore heart and shells into the sea.

And all the night I sat alone
Upon a cold and naked stone,
And to the waters made my moan:

O, cruel waves! O, mocking sea!
Within thy breast can pity be?
Bring back my heart, my shells to me.

But still the waves beat calmly on;
For other hands their gifts were strewn,
And till the morn I sat alone.

Then came a voice most soft and still,
That did the air like perfume fill,
And all my waiting spirit thrill:

"The fount of Love eternal dwells
Within the sea;
Thither the waves thy treasure bore,
To guard for thee.
Embraced within its clasping shells,
That heart of thine,
At last, to pearl-like beauty grown,
A gem shall shine.
Earth's poisonous air thy lovely shells
Had dimmed erelong,
Thy heart grown restless, and have strayed
On with the throng.
Say, from their calm and peaceful home—
Their native sea—
Shall I bring back thy heart, thy shells,
To moan to thee?"

Gladly I answered to the wave,
As it my weary feet did lave,
"Nay, keep, O keep the gifts ye gave."

And still beside the brimming sea,
Whose bright waves break in melody,
I sit, and hear them sing to me.

For other lands I have no care—
No sea of earth hath waves so fair,
My treasure and my heart are there.

ELIZABETH BARRETT BROWNING.

SOFTLY at eve went down thy sun,
And o'er thy sky the night begun.
The birds that cheered the golden day,
With gentle murmurs, hid away;
And yet thy days go on—go on.*

Palsied to silence grew thy tongue,
That to the world so sweetly sung,
The hand upon thy bosom slept
That from thy lyre such music swept;
And yet thy days go on—go on.

"The world goes whispering to its own;"
The bird of sweetest song has flown,
And friends that loved thee sigh and say,
Dear heart, that sang itself away!
And yet thy days go on—go on.

* See Mrs. Browning's "De Profundis."

Thy past is goldened by the sun—
A peak he loves to shine upon;
We fondly look, and scarce can deem
It is the past; for it doth seem
So fit thy days should still go on.

Thy life went forward with the sun,
And all is light. O, life begun
Not to be ended! Dawning bliss,
And joy that shall not end like this,
And days that ever shall go on!

Upon thy head the thorn-wreath brown
Is changed to joy's immortal crown;
Banished thy spirit's misery;
The snowy vesture is for thee,
Whose days in peace go on—go on.

While suffering and life were one,
In trust and song thy days went on;
Through nights made cold by chilling frost,
Through days whose light and bloom were lost,
Still thankfully thy days went on.

And having from thy life-well drawn
The drops of bitter, one by one,
There springeth from its fountain up
The sweetest freshness for thy cup;
And thus thy days go on—go on.

THE HARP OF THE SEA.

The first message transmitted across the Atlantic telegraph was, "Glory to God in the highest, on earth peace, good-will to men!"

WILD, harsh, and discordant, the song earth was singing—
The drum-beat of hatred swelled loud on the air;
Red hands to the breeze the red banner was flinging,
'Mid curses, that froze on her lips, Mercy's prayer.
From nation to nation the challenge was sounding,
It wakened an echo from fettered and free;
But while with the war-cry the earth was resounding,
The angel of Peace hung his harp in the sea.

Far, far 'neath the waves from the tempests controlling,
Where the sea-weed is growing the white bones among,
Though above it the waves are incessantly rolling,
In stillness it singeth its beautiful song.

And list! comes a whisper, "Peace, peace through the ocean—
How like to the voice that once stilled Galilee!
And the earth, charmed to rest from its tempest commotion,
Is singing "Peace! peace!" on the harp of the sea.

The drum-beat is silent; the love-notes of blessing
Are swelling, like Sabbath bells, sweet on the air;
A flag, the good-will of the nations expressing,
Pure hands have unfurled, 'mid the anthem and prayer.
From nation to nation the glad song is sounding,
It waketh an echo from fettered and free,
"All glory to God!" through the earth is resounding,
And "Good-will to men!" sings the harp of the sea.

"Peace! good-will to men!" 't is the hand of an angel
That wakes from the harp-string that beautiful strain:
"All glory to God!" is the blessèd evangel—
"To God in the highest, who cometh to reign!"

And hark! from the land of the dark and be-
nighted
There crieth a voice, holy watchman, to thee;
O, weary not, rest not till all lands, united,
Sing "Glory to God!" on the harp of the sea.

BEAUTIFUL FEET—LITTLE HATTIE.

Beautiful feet!
Small and dainty, but very fleet;
Shod with the morning sunshine,
  Bathed in the morning dew,
Making the sweetest music,
  As in and out they flew—
Out and away o'er the valley,
  Up by the hill-side spring,
Bearing about our treasure,
  The dearest and loveliest thing.
O, the glow of the sunshine was richer
  Wherever her footsteps fell,
And all things rare and lovely
  Acknowledged her magical spell.

Beautiful lips!
Touched with the morning's finger-tips;
Asking the strangest questions,
  Singing the sweetest strain—

How often ye pause and listen,
  Wishing to hear it again!
Calling the names of the household
  Lovingly, day by day;
Tenderly naming them over,
  The dear ones, far away;
All sounds were sweeter, blended
  With the richness of her tone—
Beautiful lips, whose music
  For evermore hath flown.

Beautiful eyes!
Filled with the light of Paradise;
Dark with their depth of meaning,
  Like a deeply-bedded well,
Where only the lights of heaven
  In softest glory dwell:
Alas! that the beauty should vanish
  From any thing so divine—
That the lip should lose its laughter,
  And the eye should cease to shine!

Beautiful feet!
Walking forever the golden street;

Shod with the fadeless sunshine,
  Bathed in the living stream,
Whose waves of crystal beauty
  Have brightened many a dream.
Beautiful lips, that are singing
  A holier, sweeter strain:
In the glorious land of immortals
  Its music shall thrill thee again.
Beautiful eyes, whose brightness
  No sorrow can ever pale,
That look on the face of the Father
  With never a dimming vail.
O, the beauty hath risen to glory,
  Eternal and wondrous, divine;
The star hath been kindled in newness,
  Forever and ever to shine.
And, passing the mystical river
  That rolleth so darkly between
This land and the country forever
Arrayed in perennial green,
As we tread, with the glide of a spirit,
  Those upper lands, blooming and sweet,
We shall hear the dear voice, full of gladness,
  The falling of beautiful feet.

PATRIOTIC PIECES.

HYMN FOR A FLAG-RAISING.

God of our patriotic sires,
Guarding our freedom's altar-fires,
Whose ever-glowing heat inspires
  The life-blood in each vein,
To-day this flag we raise on high,
And swear, beneath the eternal sky,
For it to live, for it to die—
  Its honor to maintain.

O'er many a well-fought battle-plain,
Where, from the hero's quivering vein,
The glowing blood was poured like rain,
  This banner proudly waved;
And, 'mid the cannon's thunderous boom,
Amid the war-smoke's hovering gloom,
It shed its glorious light and bloom,
  Until the field was saved.

In every breeze its folds have curled,
Its stars have lighted all the world
Since first it proudly was unfurled,
  The ensign of the free;
And now, amid the song and prayer,
With hands to do and hearts to dare,
We proudly fling it to the air,
  And trust, O God, to thee.

We trust to thee, O Freedom's sire!
Each nerve and throbbing vein inspire,
Each heart with holy ardor fire,
  As here we swear again,
While waves our flag triumphantly,
For it to live, for it to die;
And though the traitor hosts defy,
  Its honor to maintain.

OUR SOLDIERS.

Beneath each homestead's sheltering roof,
  Around each family tree,
They grew, the sons our mothers bore—
  The offspring of the free.

A noble race of clear-eyed men,
  With loving hearts and true,
The warm clasp of whose hand spoke that
  Which traitor never knew.

Whose sinewy limbs were knit with strength,
  With grace in every line,
And through whose veins the blood was poured
  Like floods of eastern wine.

Calm beamed each eye, the native plains
  And home possessions o'er;
Light fell each footstep on the turf,
  Around the homestead door.

Clear rang the voice of manly song
  Beside each dancing stream,
And sweetly fell the tones that thrilled
  Full many a maiden's dream.

Till when at last on Southern winds
  The boast of traitors came,
We learned that 'neath each quiet breast
  There throbbed a heart of flame.

And then from out the hovering shade
  Of the old homestead tree,
They went—the sons our mothers love—
  The armies of the free.

They knew thy voice, O Freedom's God!
  They heard their country call,
And hastened with their strength to save—
  To save, or bravely fall.

A million eager hands they raised
  To bear the flag on high,
And set its stars in gold again
  Upon the Southern sky.

Then—O, not to each sheltering roof,
  Not 'neath each homestead tree,
Shall come again our mothers' sons,
  The honored, loved, and free.

Their forms shall sleep in many a vale,
  By many a foreign stream;
The manly song and tones of love
  Thrill but the maiden's dream.

But they shall live, e'en though they fall,
  The noble and the brave—
Live wheresoe'er shall float the flag
  They gave their lives to save.

THE DAY OF EMANCIPATION.

JANUARY 1, 1863.

DAWNING at last! the morning sun is beaming,
  Glad and expectant, o'er the eastern hill;
Dawning at last! adown the hill-side streaming,
  Until the splendor all the vale doth fill.

Dawning at last! through flame and smoke of battle,
  O'er faces pallid as their bed of snow;
Dawning at last! O, day whose earlier dawning
  Had saved our land these tears and weeds of woe.

O'er trodden field and ruined home and city,
  O'er whitening bones and hearts bereft and sad,
Scenes over which the angels weep in pity,
  Thy sunlight falleth beautiful and glad.

Ay, beautiful o'er yonder hut thy dawning,
  Beside whose door a dark-browed infant plays,
There 's freedom for the child this New-Year's
    morning,
  A crown of manhood woven from its rays.

Freedom for child and sire through all the nation,
  Freedom to be a man and claim his own—
To claim the soul for which Christ made oblation,
  His own right hand, his wife, his child, his home.

Ah! precious blood of father, friend, and brother,
  That stained the flowers on many a Southern
    plain!
Ah! bitter tears of sister, wife, and mother,
  So sadly shed! ye were not shed in vain.

For lo! from out this river of baptism
  A nation comes, regenerate and pure,
The buried manhood of a race hath risen,
  To sit with men and God, eternal and secure.

THE RAVELED SHEET.

SUGGESTED WHILE RAVELING OLD "HOMESPUN" LINEN INTO LINT FOR THE HOSPITALS.

"'T is ever thus war ravels out
The soft, white web of peace."

I.

SPIN, spin, spin!
All day the cottage wheel,
With sweet, domestic hum,
Whirled round and round, the lengthening thread
Passed 'neath her steady thumb;
The soft wind fanned her fair young cheek,
Where the crimson went and came;
Was it the south wind's gentle touch
That dashed her brow with flame?

Weave, weave, weave!
From out her fingers white
All day the shuttle flew,
And in the web that flaxen thread
Was woven through and through;

And a thoughtful look came to her face
  As the measure grew complete,
And her fingers quivered as she cut
  From the loom her bridal sheet.

Ah, blessed toil! ah, holy love!
  That made that toil so sweet,
That from the whirring of the wheel
  Strung music so complete;
That made that bridal web so blest
  Till it was worn and old,
That hallowed many a little form
  She gathered to her fold.

II.

Ah, patient toil! ah, tender love!
  That filled that toil with pain,
That brought the tears from gentle eyes
  In swiftly-falling rain.
Love wrought with joy the fleecy web
  Love ravels out to-day,
With hands that falter at their task,
  And lips that, yearning, pray.

One by one the white shreds fall
  From the wrinkled fingers brown,
One by one from the rosy tips
  Of the child-hand softly down;
One thinking of the happy day
  When her young heart was won,
And of the changes that had passed
  Since first those threads were spun,
And of the manly soldier's brow
  They may be bound upon.

One dreaming of a blissful day,
  With many a trembling fear,
With many a prayer that God would haste
  Its dawning, still more near,
When war should pass and peace should smile,
  And he return again
Whose love had won her maiden heart,
  To mingled love and pain.

In vain—God help thy constant heart—
  In vain thy dreams of him;
Thy golden hair shall lose its gleam,
  Thy eyes be old and dim,

And of the web hope spun for thee
  Not e'en a shred remain
To bind about thy wounded heart
  Ere ye shall meet again.

All wars shall pass, the tide of blood
  Forever more shall cease;
Upon the calm, dead face of Time
  Shall rest the smile of peace,
And from the bosom of the earth
  Be gathered up her slain
To immortality of life,
  Where ye shall meet again.

For where his banner cast its shade,
  'Mid smoke, and shot, and shell,
'Mid armies' tramp and cannon's boom,
  Thy loved one fought and fell,
Covered with wounds most bravely won,
  And honors borne so well,
Filled with a love for land and thee,
  Whose deepness—who can tell?
Low sighs the wind above his grave
  'Neath the magnolia-tree,

And, swaying on the fragrant boughs,
  The ring-dove mourns for thee,
While sweetly singing to his sleep
  Flows on the Tennessee.

III.

Fair was the web Love wove for thee
  As yonder drift of snow;
But raveled are its threads to-day—
  Thou naked in thy woe;
But blest, who in thy country's need
  Spared not that form of' thine,
But bared thy bosom that thy scarf
  Her wounded breast might twine.

Ay, blest, thou maiden young and fair,
  Thy dreams of love to thee;
But blest with sweeter, richer joy
  Thy coming years shall be,
When from each crimson drop that from
  Thy quivering heart was wrung,
A freeman, clad with grace and strength,
  To god-like life hath sprung,

And forth upon the morning breeze
  Is borne the jubilee
That swelleth from a million hearts—
  The birth-song of the free.

THE END.

www.ingramcontent.com/pod-product-compliance
Lightning Source LLC
LaVergne TN
LVHW011229110826
845150LV00006B/1589
9781425515386